THE FOUR BRANCHES OF THE MABINOGI
PEDEIR KEINC Y MABINOGI

GW00471809

The Four Branches of the Mabinogi

of the Mabinogi

Pedeir Keinc y Mabinogi

Sioned Davies

First impression—1993

ISBN 1 85902 005 4

© Sioned Davies

This volume is published with the support of the
Welsh Arts Council.

Printed in Wales
at the Gomer Press, Llandysul, Dyfed

CONTENTS

PREFACE

This volume is a translation and adaptation of *Pedeir Keinc y Mabinogi* (Pantycelyn Press, 1989), which was awarded the Welsh Arts Council award for Literary Criticism in 1990. The Welsh language volume was published in the *Llên y Llenor* series, a series intended to introduce the classics of Welsh literature to a wider audience. Although scholarly apparatus has been included in this English version, the main aim remains the same.

I am very grateful to Pantycelyn Press and to Professor J. E. Caerwyn Williams (the editor of the series) for permission to publish an English version of the 1989 volume. I am also grateful to my colleague, Dr Dafydd Johnston, for his many constructive comments. Finally, I owe special thanks to Richard for his encouragement and patience. This English version, too, is for my parents.

Sioned Davies

1 THE BACKGROUND

Pedeir Keinc y Mabinogi (The Four Branches of the Mabinogi) form part of a collection of eleven medieval Welsh prose tales known generally as *The Mabinogion* [Jones and Jones 1949; Mac Cana 1977]. This collective title was first given to the tales by Lady Charlotte Guest when she translated them into English during the nineteenth century [Guest 1849]. However, the word *mabinogion* occurs only once in the original text, and even then it seems to be an error. Yet it has become a useful term to describe this corpus of prose tales, although we should not perceive them as a unified collection of any kind. The *Pedeir Keinc* (The Four Branches) are the only tales that have a true claim to the title *Mabinogi*; it is apparent that they stand independently and form a special group. The earliest complete text of the *Pedeir Keinc* is found in the manuscript known as *Llyfr Gwyn Rhydderch* (The White Book of Rhydderch), written about 1350, and *Llyfr Coch Hergest* (The Red Book of Hergest), written about 1400 [Huws 1991; G. Charles-Edwards 1979-80]. Portions of the second and third branches appear in Peniarth Manuscript 6 which is earlier than the *Llyfr Gwyn* by about one hundred years. However, there is general agreement that the texts are much older than the manuscripts, and the consensus of opinion is that the *Pedeir Keinc* appeared in a written form for the first time between about 1050 and 1120 [T. M. Charles-Edwards 1970; Sims-Williams 1991]. It is possible to go back even further—it would seem that the tales, or parts of them, were transmitted orally for centuries before they were safeguarded in manuscript form and therefore the material, or part of it certainly, can claim to have its roots in the distant past.

The art of the storyteller has been an important social art in every country throughout the centuries. Wales is no exception. A verse from a Welsh ballad, 'The Old Man of the Woods', by Ellis Roberts, claims:

> Dwedai hen ŵr llwyd o'r gornel
> 'Gan fy nhad mi glywes chwedel,
> A chan ei daid y clywsai yntau
> Ac ar ei ôl mi gofiais innau'.
> (An old gray man from the corner said
> 'From my father I heard a tale,

And from his grandfather he had heard it
And after him I have remembered it too'.)

The *Pedeir Keinc* belong in essence to this world of storytelling—they are tales that were transmitted orally for centuries before arriving at their present 'final' form. Yet they are not tales that were transmitted informally from father to son within the family unit, but were part of the repertoire of the *cyfarwydd*, the professional storyteller. Although little is known for certain about the *cyfarwydd* in medieval Wales, we can surmise that his work involved entertaining the court with his tales, tales such as the *Mabinogion*. In Ireland it seems that the composition of both prose and poetry was undertaken by the same man—the craft of the storyteller was linked to that of the *fili*, the poet, although storytelling was not one of his main functions [Mac Cana 1980]. In Wales there is no direct evidence regarding the relationship between the *bardd* (poet) and *cyfarwydd* (storyteller), although it would appear that they belonged to the same privileged class of learned men at least at one time in their history. Yet it is difficult to explain why there are no references to the *cyfarwydd* in the medieval Welsh law texts for example. Perhaps it is because verse was the medium of the earliest tales and that the author recomposed metrical tales when he recorded *Pedeir Keinc y Mabinogi* and their like on vellum.

It must be remembered, of course, that storytelling has been one of the main functions of the poet in Europe throughout the centuries. The convention in most Indo-European countries was that a story should be narrated in verse. The *Iliad*, the *Odyssey*, and Vergil's *Aenid* are metrical narratives; the bulk of Anglo-Saxon literature was in alliterative verse—the epic *Beowulf*, the shorter epic *Waldhere*, the heroic poems of *Finn*, *Deor* and *Widsith*. On the other hand, early English *prose* literature tends to be religious, historical or philosophical in its appeal. In France, non-didactic literature was in metrical form until the end of the twelfth century—Old French epics such as the *Song of Roland* were composed in assonant verse; the series of French romances produced in the third quarter of the twelfth century were versified. It would seem, therefore, that Celtic narrative literature follows a totally different pattern, for in Ireland and Wales (and in Scandinavia too) the earliest surviving narrative texts are in prose. The nature of the poetic tradition was different amongst the Celts too—verse was mainly, if not wholly, employed for elegy and eulogy. Throughout the centuries great honour was bestowed on the poet and he was regarded as a craftsman of words and the preserver of tradition. The names of the earliest poets composing in the Welsh language have survived—Aneirin and Taliesin—but nothing is known of the authors of medieval Welsh prose. Even today the Chair and Crown at the National Eisteddfod of Wales are given for poetic compositions and the National Anthem of Wales reflects the particular status confirmed on poets:

> Mae hen wlad fy nhadau yn annwyl i mi,
> Gwlad beirdd a chantorion, enwogion o fri...
> (The land of my fathers is dear to me,
> The land of poets and singers, of great renown...)

The situation in medieval Wales was, therefore, a complex one, as emphasised by Brynley Roberts [1984:212]. Bardic triads affirm a strong connection between *cyfarwyddyd* and *barddoniaeth* (poetry) in medieval Wales:

> Tri pheth a berthyn ar wr wrth gerdd davawd:
> Kerdd, a chof, a chyfarwyddyd...
> Tri chyfarwyddyd yssydd: hengerdd, ystoriav, a barddoniaeth.
> (Three things pertain to the poet:
> Poetry, and memory, and cyfarwyddyd...
> There are three types of cyfarwyddyd: early poetry,
> stories, and poetry.) [Williams and Jones 1934:134]

The terms *hengerdd* (early poetry) and *barddoniaeth* (poetry) suggest a metrical form, while the nature of *ystoriav* (stories) is uncertain. According to another triad:

> Tri pheth a beir y gerdawr vot yn amyl:
> kyfarwydyt ystoryaeu, a bardoniaeth, a hengerd.
> (Three things give a poet amplitude:
> knowledge of stories, and poetry, and early poetry)
> [Williams and Jones 1934:18]

while a later medieval treatise (found only in an English version) states:

> The three memories of the bard are:
> knowledge of history, language and genealogies.
> [Bromwich 1974:52]

It would seem, therefore, that the original meaning of *cyfarwyddyd* was not tale, but rather 'traditional lore' or traditional learning which was necessary for society to function [Roberts 1988:62]. The term itself is connected etymologically with 'knowledge, guidance, perception', and the *cyfarwydd* was 'the guide, well-informed person, expert' [Mac Cana 1980:139]. Various classes of learned men would have been responsible for the different aspects of *cyfarwyddyd,* including the lawyers, mediciners and bards. The bardic *cyfarwyddyd* would have been transmitted in verse form, while other material would have been transmitted in the form of oral narrative. Although originally these narratives were intended to be informative, they came to be viewed more and more as entertainment, hence the later semantic development of *cyfarwyddyd* in Middle Welsh where it is commonly used for 'story, narrative' and *cyfarwydd* for 'storyteller' [Roberts 1988:62-63]. Or as suggested by Mac Cana [1980:139], what may have happened is that the semantic range of the word *cyfarwydd* used as a quasi-literary term became gradually narrowed until in the end it was virtually confined to one, and that a lesser one, of its older connotations.

It is certain that the author of *Pedeir Keinc y Mabinogi* drew on traditional sources for his material. He states this categorically on two occasions:

Branwen A hynny a dyweit y kyuarwydyd hwnn eu kyfranc wy. 'Y gwyr a gychwynwys o Iwerdon,' yw hwnnw. [p.47]
(And that is what this *cyfarwyddyd* says; that is their tale, 'The men who set out from Ireland'.) [p.40]*

Math A herwyd y dyweit y kyuarwydyt, ef a uu arglwyd wedy hynny ar Wyned. [p.92]
(And according to the *cyfarwyddyd* he was lord thereafter over Gwynedd.) [p.75]

Throughout the centuries, storytellers had presumably selected and rationalized the oral material so that the tales were suitable for entertaining princes and courtiers. It could therefore be argued that *Pedeir Keinc y Mabinogi* are the work of many heads and hands—they are tales that developed independently of any single specific 'author'. Then, however, some individual came and 'wrote down' these tales for the first time ever. Transmission from an oral to a written medium would be a very complicated process. Did the storyteller dictate his tales, or was he able to write them down in person? In either case, the

---

*All quotations from *Pedeir Keinc y Mabinogi* are taken from I.Williams 1930, and the English translation from Jones and Jones 1949.

redactor would have to slow his pace, thereby losing his train of thought perhaps, although if the storyteller knew the tale word for word there seems to be no reason why the written copy should not be an almost exact reproduction of the oral tale. The general consensus, however, is that *Pedeir Keinc y Mabinogi* are the work of an individual, not a reporter's transcript of a spoken tale, but the product of one mind, a deliberate artistic piece of literature. According to W.J. Gruffydd [1953:2]:

> If the material from which it is built bore at one stage the distinctive marks of oral recitation, the *Mabinogi,* as we know it, has shed most of them.

I hope to show before the end of the discussion that this statement is not entirely true. Ifor Williams, too, is of the opinion that the tales are the creation of one particular author [1930:xii]:

> Yr oedd y gwahanol straeon a asiwyd ynghyd yn y Ceinciau hyn yn bod ganrifoedd lawer, fe ddichon, cyn i ryw gyfarwydd eu cyfuno, a'u golygu nes gwneud un chwedl ohonynt.
> (The various tales that were welded together in the Branches existed, perhaps, centuries before some storyteller unified and edited them, forming one tale out of them.)

This is the general consensus of opinion, therefore, regarding authorship of *Pedeir Keinc y Mabinogi.* Yet, it is difficult to ascertain how much of the work of the final author is reflected in our text. Was he responsible for bringing the four tales together for the first time, or did they already exist in such a form in the oral tradition? Also was it his aim to create a complete artistic whole, or merely to record a collection of independent tales that bore a loose relationship one with the other? We will examine these problems in more detail when discussing the structure of *Pedeir Keinc y Mabinogi.*

And who was this author? It has been suggested many times that he was a cleric [Mac Cana 1958:182-183; Goetinck 1988]. The monasteries were important centres of learning at this time in Wales, and emphasis is placed time and time again in the *Pedeir Keinc* on the virtues and good qualities of the characters. Pwyll's chastity is emphasised; Manawydan's patience; Rhiannon and Branwen both suffer like martyrs, knowing full well that they personally have done no wrong. And in every tale, good overcomes evil. It must be remembered, too, that members of important Welsh families often entered the monasteries and such people would be familiar with the oral entertainment of the day. There has been one attempt, hitherto, to link the name of a particular family with the *Pedeir Keinc,* that being the family of Bishop Sulien, a man described in *Brut y Tywysogion* (The Chronicle of Princes) as

y doethaf ar kreuydussaf o esgyb y brytanyeid ar kloduorussaf herwyd dysc y disgyblyon ay blwyueu.
(The wisest and most religious of British bishops and the most renowned because of the knowledge of his disciples and his parishioners.)
[Thomas Jones 1941:24]

Having spent thirteen years in Ireland, Sulien returned to Wales and established a school of learning at Llanbadarn Fawr. He was subsequently elected bishop of St. David's. Nothing of his work remains, at least nothing that actually bears his name. However, much of the work of his sons still stands today, and bears witness to the state of learning in Ceredigion before the Norman Conquest [Lapidge 1973-74]. Sulien's son Rhigyfarch seems to have been the most distinguished for his learning. He compiled a psalter and martyrology, and it was he who was responsible for the *Vita Davidis* (Life of Saint David), c.1093. There is a strong Irish influence on the latter and it could be argued that most of the Irish hagiographical material incorporated in it was obtained from Sulien, whose stay in Ireland was most probably spent in one of the Irish monasteries in which the native secular literature and lives of the saints were being composed. According to Proinsias Mac Cana [1958:184-7], Sulien could have set about re-moulding certain Welsh traditions with the help of material borrowed from Irish texts; or he may have provided the 'matière d'Irlande' for his son Rhigyfarch to work upon, material that is very apparent in the second branch *Branwen.* As Mac Cana has pointed out [1958:186-187], we have here two texts—*Branwen* and *Vita Davidis*—one secular and in Welsh, one hagiographical and in Latin, both written at the same period and both deriving much of their content from Irish sources. The *Vita Davidis* is known to have been written by Rhigyfarch; the author of *Branwen,* on the other hand, is unknown—a cleric, perhaps, who came from Dyfed. A reasonable case could therefore be made for attributing *Branwen*—and the *Pedeir Keinc* as a whole—to Rhigyfarch or his father Sulien, or to both in collaboration. However, Sims-Williams has argued that the evidence for vernacular Irish literary influence on early medieval Welsh literature is very tenuous, and regards medieval Irish literature as a rich and indispensable quarry for analogues rather than for sources [1982:257; 1977-8]. So the question of authorship of *Pedeir Keinc y Mabinogi* is still very much an open question.

It must be remembered, of course, that writing in the Middle Ages was mainly restricted to a few scholars with a clerical education. Apart from members of a *clas,* that is a body of canons attached to a mother church [G. Williams 1976:17], there may have been other groups of 'literati' capable of composing such tales as the *Pedeir Keinc.* Some clerics, for example, were associated with the king's court and were responsible for writing down the actual legal cases discussed:

> Tri ryw wassannaeth ysyd y offeirat llys yn dadleuoed: dileu pob dadyl a darffo y thervynu o'r [r]ol; eil yw cadw ynn yscriuennedic hyt varnn pob dadyl hynny teruynner; trydyd yw bot yn barawt ac yn diuedw wrth reit y brenhin y wnneuthur llythyreu ac eu darllein.[Williams and Powell 1961:13]
> (The court priest has three kinds of service to give in sessions: to delete from the roll every case which has been determined; second is to keep in writing up to judgement every case until it is determined; third is to be ready and unintoxicated at the King's need, to write letters and to read them.) [Jenkins 1986:12]

It would seem, therefore, that the court priest was some sort of clerk to the king—he held a secretarial office. At the court of Athelstan, a king who greatly influenced Hywel Dda and his laws, it is believed that there were clerks trained in the art of formal composition, and that a writing office was attached to the king's court. Perhaps a similar system existed in the Welsh court at this time—the chief clerk was the *offeiryat,* while his pupils—the *ysgolheigyon*—were his staff:

> Llety yr offeirat a'r yscolheigyonn yw ty caplan y tref.
> (The lodgings for the priest and clerks is the townland chaplain's house.) [Williams and Powell 1961:9]

These would surely be taught to read and write in order that they might later carry out the duties of an *offeiryat.* Moreover, these men would be in daily contact with the life in a Welsh court, and would surely be acquainted with the poetry and tales of the time. It may well be, therefore, that our 'author' is to be found amongst the *ysgolheigyon* or *offeiriaid* at the king's court.

There was also another class of 'literati' closely associated with the court and its customs—the justices and lawyers. *Llyfr Blegywryd* (The Book of Blegywryd) gives us an account of the training demanded of

15

a court judge—he was obliged to reside at court for one year, observing the laws and customs of the court, listening to trials and verdicts. This training must also have included reading, if not writing too:

> Tri pheth a berthyn wrth vrawdwr... trydyd yw, yr hynn a dospartho trwy varnn, y gatarnhav trwy wystyl a brawtlyuyr, ot ymwystlir ac ef...
> (Three things pertain to the judge... third, that which he gives out through judgement, he must confirm by pledge and lawbook if he is challenged) [Williams and Powell 1961:17]

These men were not drawn from the ranks of the Church:

> Tri dyn yssyd ny digawn vn ohonunt bot yn vrawdwr teilwg o gyfreith ... Eil yw dyn eglwyssic, rwymedic wrth vrdeu kyssegredic, neu wrth greuyd.....
> (There are three men who are not allowed to be judges worthy of the law... Second is a man of the Church, bound by holy orders or by religion....) [Williams and Powell 1961:104]

According to Saunders Lewis [1932:36], the lawyers gave to Welsh medieval literature a certain discipline and design, the characteristics of a 'finished' composition, economy of style. Such features are prominent in *Pedeir Keinc y Mabinogi,* and throughout the tales there are many references to legal terms and concepts [Ellis 1928; T.M. Charles-Edwards 1978]. It is true that these legal terms rise, as a rule, from the everyday life of the community, and that their usage is not always proof of familiarity with special legal language. Yet it does seem valid to ask whether a lawyer could have been responsible for writing *Pedeir Keinc y Mabinogi.* Morfydd Owen [1974:242] goes so far as to say that certain passages in the law tracts bear characteristics of the narrative storytelling techniques that are common in historical and mythological prose and that there is not such a great gap between the art of the storyteller and the art of the editors of the law books.

A member of a Welsh *clas*; a cleric at court; a lawyer—each one of these could have written *Pedeir Keinc y Mabinogi.* Or there may well be another possibility—the author may have been a *cyfarwydd/* poet educated at a church school. A detailed examination of the text will, I hope, bring us a little closer, not to solving the problem of authorship finally, but to arriving at a better understanding of the nature and character of our author.

2 STRUCTURE

Pedeir Keinc y Mabinogi—The Title

The four tales under consideration are generally known today by the title *Pedeir Keinc y Mabinogi*. It should be noted that this particular title does not occur in the manuscripts at all—it is a modern title, reflecting the attempt of modern scholars to perceive unity in the four tales [Davies 1990]. It is true that a similar colophon ends each tale in *Llyfr Gwyn Rhydderch*:

> Ac yuelly y teruyna y geing honn or mabinogi
> (And so ends this branch of the mabinogi)

—giving rise to the present day title. But there is no firm evidence that these are branches of the same *mabinogi*. Indeed, the reference to *Mabinogi Mynweir a Mynord* at the end of the third tale suggests that it was an independent *mabinogi*. There is no reason either to believe that there were originally *four* branches, especially when we remember the importance of triadic grouping in early Welsh society. Therefore, due to the paucity of the manuscript tradition, care is needed when analysing and generalising. Turning our attention to *Llyfr Coch Hergest* we find the evidence is slightly different. Here, before copying the first branch, the scribe has included the words:

> llyma dechreu mabinogi
> (this is the beginning of a mabinogi)

and the following titles are given to the remaining three tales:

> llyma yr eil geinc or mabinogi
> llyma y dryded geinc or mabinogi
> honn yw y bedwared geinc or mabinogi
> (this is the second branch of the mabinogi
> this is the third branch of the mabinogi
> this is the fourth branch of the mabinogi)

According to this evidence each branch is part of the same *mabinogi*. Perhaps the scribe was drawing his own conclusions having seen the text of the *Llyfr Gwyn* or a similar manuscript. There is certainly no proof that there were only *four* branches originally; indeed, *Llyfr Coch Hergest* suggests that there were more than four branches. The scribe begins with the words:

17

llyma dechreu mabinogi
(this is the beginning of a mabinogi)

and one would expect him to end the sequence with a similar formula:

*llyma teruyn y mabinogi
(this is the end of the mabinogi)

—especially since he usually marks very clearly when his tales are at an end, for example:

> Ar chwedyl hwnn a elwir kyfranc llud a lleuelys. Ac uelly y teruynha.
> (And this tale is called the encounter of Lludd and Llefelys. And this is how it ends.)
>
> Ar chwedyl hwnn a elwir breudwyt maxen wledic amherawdyr ruuein.
> Ac yman y mae teruyn arnaw.
> (And this tale is called the dream of Maxen Wledig the emperor of Rome. And here it ends.)

However, at the end of the Four Branches the Red Book scribe makes no such declaration. It is difficult to come to any definite conclusions regarding the number of branches. Let us examine, therefore, in more detail the description of these tales—*ceinc or mabinogi* (branch of the *mabinogi*). *Cainc* usually means a branch, a secondary stem arising from the trunk or bough of a tree. It can also mean a twisted thread (in a rope). There is also a further possible meaning, namely a song or tune. This last meaning is interesting from the point of view of the text—were these originally tales to be sung? Evidence from other countries points to the importance of music in an oral performance. Little is known of the performance of narrative tales in medieval Wales, but surely a musical context cannot be ruled out. However, scholars have tended to interpret *cainc* as 'part', 'portion', 'branch', and have therefore assumed that the four tales are closely related.

Many have attempted to interpret the word *mabinogi*. 'Juvenile tales, tales written to while away the time of young chieftains' according to William Owen-Pughe [Stephens 1876:396,416]; 'the traditional material—mythical, heroic, genealogical—which [the *Mabinog* or bardic apprentice] had to acquire is Alfred Nutt's opinion [1910:33]. More recently Eric P. Hamp has argued on linguistic grounds that the meaning is a collection of material pertaining to the god Maponos or Mabon [1975]. In the tale of *Culhwch ac Olwen*, Mabon is stolen from the bed of his mother Modron (Matrona, the

Divine Mother), and indeed W. J. Gruffydd has attempted to identify Mabon with Pryderi and Modron with Rhiannon [1953]. However, the general consensus is that *mabinogi* contains the element *mab,* and that the meaning is youth or the story of youth. This is confirmed by the fact that the word appears synonymously with *maboliaeth* (youth) and as a translation of the Latin *infantia* (youth) [Evans 1907:xxvi]. If we are to accept this interpretation, then we must ask whose youthful exploits are related in the tales? Ifor Williams has argued that the original hero was Pryderi—he is the only character to appear in all four tales [1930:xliv-l]. In Williams' opinion, the first branch is the original *mabinogi* and the other tales are developments on this branch. W. J. Gruffydd went further and argued for a much more formal relationship between the four branches [1953]. He argued that originally the tales formed four chapters in the biography of the hero Pryderi—his mysterious birth, his youth, his imprisonment and his death. He showed that these categories are to be found in Irish tales, and indeed one cannot disagree that the *Compert* (Conception), *Macgnimartha* (Youthful Exploits), *Indarba* (Exile) and *Aided* (Death) are types of tales found in Irish. However, as Brynley Roberts has emphasised, there is no evidence to suppose that they formed a heroic 'biography', and it is easier to believe that W. J. Gruffydd himself created the pattern on the basis of which he re-structured the original hypothetical forms of the tales [1980:xiv].

Mabinogi may, therefore, have originally referred to the story of Pryderi's youth. However, he can hardly be described as the hero of the Four Branches. He is a major character in the first and third branch, but his role in the second and the fourth is minimal. I would tend to agree with Brynley Roberts who argues that Pryderi's role is to bring together various traditions rather than provide a basis for them [1980:xv]. *Mabinogi* in this context, therefore, may best be defined as 'a combination of tales', 'a collection of more or less related adventures' [Ford 1977:3-4].

The Structure of Oral Tales

To my mind many scholars in the past have placed too much emphasis on attempting to find a close relationship between the four tales, and have perhaps neglected the virtues and art of the individual branches. There is, of course, a relationship between the tales; there are narrative echoes and cross-references throughout and the author moves chronologically through the events—there is obviously too great a link between the four branches for them to be considered as totally independent tales [Bollard 1975]. Yet, there are inconsistencies and deficiencies in the plot. Rather than look for a basic unity in the four branches, it is more helpful to accept them as a collection of adventures or episodes that bear some sort of relationship with each other and are therefore *ceinciau* (branches), but that have no ambitious pattern behind them [Ford 1977:3-4]. It must be remembered that we are dealing with medieval tales, and as emphasised by R.M.Jones [1986:175]:

> a sympathetic reading and a satisfactory reaction to the *Gestalt* of a medieval tale is prejudiced unless we have examined what may have been the premises in the middle ages. Ideas of what constructed a whole in medieval times were somewhat different from our contemporary prejudices...

These tales, or parts of them, were at one stage narrated orally, and it can be argued that the influence of an oral mnemonic structure is to be seen on the written texts. It is generally held that an oral tale has a chronological and episodic structure, with one strand to the narrative [Olrik 1965:137]. Such features are surely linked to the role of the memory in oral narrative, as noted by Rosenberg in his discussion of American folk sermons [1990:154]:

> Memory... exerts pressure on the sequence of clauses within a sentence. Clauses tend to be generated chronologically, matching their sequence to the sequence of the sentences describing them. Memory performs better with temporally arranged sentences... Clearly the events have an effect on the way sentences are organized. The simplest sort of plot structure characterizes the stories in the sermons: a straightforward single-strand narrative, each episode of which is introduced by such formulas as 'after a while' and 'by and by'.

Such features are prominent in the *Pedeir Keinc,* so that although the tales are by now in a literary form, the oral background has left its mark on their structure. Hildegard Tristram draws attention to this point [1989:427]:

> In the Insular world, writing as a new technique of verbal communication did not give rise to entirely new modes of literary expression. Its effects lay in the sophistication of the inherited pre-literary modes.

Summary of the content of the Pedeir Keinc

Before analysing the structure of the *Pedeir Keinc* it will be useful to examine the content of the tales. It should be emphasised at the outset that there are no titles to the individual tales in the manuscripts. Once again, the titles have been added by modern scholars. It is therefore misleading to refer to the branches as *Mabinogi Pwyll, Mabinogi Branwen, Mabinogi Manawydan* and *Mabinogi Math,* since according to the traditional interpretation there is only *one* mabinogi here.

The first branch tells of the tale of Pwyll Pendefig Dyfed (Pwyll Prince of Dyfed) and his encounter with Arawn, the king of Annwfn, the Otherworld. They exchange places for a year during which time Pwyll kills Hafgan, Arawn's enemy. Because of this favour a friendship develops between Pwyll and Arawn, and they send gifts to each other. Then Pwyll wins Rhiannon as a bride, but in the wedding feast Gwawl son of Clud appears and claims Rhiannon for himself. At the end of a year Pwyll succeeds in tricking Gwawl, and Pwyll and Rhiannon are married. A son is born to them but he disappears on the night of his birth. Rhiannon is accused of killing her son and is punished. Teyrnon Twrf Fliant discovers the child under strange circumstances, and he is adopted by Teyrnon and his wife. The child is given the name of Gwri Wallt Euryn (Gwri of the Golden Hair). Eventually he is restored to his father's court and is renamed Pryderi (meaning 'care'), because his mother is 'delivered of (her) care' now that her son has returned. After Pwyll's death Pryderi rules Dyfed and marries Cigfa.

The second branch tells of the family of Llŷr. Brân or Bendigeidfran is king of Britain; he has a brother, Manawydan, and a sister, Branwen; Nisien and Efnysien are their two half brothers. Matholwch, king of Ireland, comes to Wales to ask for the hand of Branwen, and they are married. Efnysien gets to know of this and insults Matholwch by destroying his horses. Brân gives gifts to pacify him, including a cauldron of restoration (when dead men are placed in the cauldron they will rise the following day, but will not have the power of speech). Having returned to Ireland a son, Gwern, is born to Branwen and Matholwch. Branwen is then punished by the Irish because of her brother Efnysien's insult to Matholwch. However, Brân and his hosts come to rescue her. Gwern, son of Matholwch, is thrown into the fire by Efnysien and the hosts of Ireland and Britain are destroyed, apart from Branwen and seven Welshmen, Pryderi and Manawydan amongst them. They follow the mortally wounded

21

Brân's instructions, and having feasted in Harlech and Gwales they bury the head of their lord Brân in the Gwynfryn (White Mound) in London.

In the third branch Pryderi gives his mother, Rhiannon, as a wife to Manawydan. An enchantment falls on Dyfed, and Manawydan and his wife, together with Pryderi and Cigfa, travel to England to seek work. Upon their return to Dyfed, Pryderi and his mother disappear in a magic fort. Manawydan succeeds in freeing them by capturing the wife of Llwyd son of Cilcoed, the magician who placed the enchantment on Dyfed to punish Rhiannon and Pryderi because of the ill-treatment of Gwawl in the first branch.

In the last branch we are told of Math son of Mathonwy, lord of Gwynedd. When he is not at war he must rest his feet in the lap of a virgin. Gilfaethwy, his nephew, falls in love with the virgin, and Gwydion, Gilfaethwy's brother, succeeds in bringing about war between Math and Pryderi in order to free the girl. Pryderi is tricked into giving Gwydion the pigs which he received as a present from Annwfn. The result of this is a bitter battle and the death of Pryderi. Gwydion and Gilfaethwy are punished by being transformed into animals for a period. Aranrhod is the new virgin offered to Math, but in her attempt to prove her virginity she gives birth to a son, Dylan, and a 'small something' that eventually develops into a boy. Later Aranrhod places three curses on her second son: he is to have neither a name, arms nor a wife, but he succeeds in spite of her. He is given the name Lleu Llaw Gyffes (Lleu of the Skilful Hand), he obtains arms, and a wife is conjured up for him out of flowers—Blodeuwedd (Flower Face). She falls in love with Gronw Pebyr and they both attempt to kill Lleu who is transformed into an eagle, but Gwydion succeeds in disenchanting him. Gronw is killed and Blodeuwedd is transformed into an owl.

Symmetrical Composition

I should now like to turn to the episodic structure of the branches and focus on a feature closely associated with oral performance, namely symmetrical composition. When the medieval storyteller narrated his tales orally, surely one of the factors that was of utmost importance to him was the length of his performance. In order to complete his recitation in a given time, the *cyfarwydd* would tend to give equal space to each of the points in his narrative. He would therefore progress from point to point with due regard for the symmetries of his story

22

[Robson 1961; Dorson 1960:32; Clover 1986]. Also it is possible that a story may have been narrated in separate sections, with the result that a particular length developed for each section, a length convenient for one session of oral delivery [Compare Lloyd-Morgan 1981:197]. However, when the work was transmitted to manuscript form, a new situation developed. Parchment was expensive and scarce; the process of writing was laborious. As a result there was always the tendency to abbreviate and to summarise when transmitting words to parchment. Often, too, a scribe would be limited to a certain amount of vellum or parchment. One could argue, therefore, that few oral tales ever reached written form in the state in which they had existed orally. Let us examine *Pedeir Keinc y Mabinogi* in the light of these comments. The branches are composed of sections, each section containing one main episode, or two or more shorter related episodes.

The First Branch
Pwyll has a tripartite structure:
1. The tale of Pwyll and Arawn   W.M. col. 1-12.27
                                         11¾ col.
2. Pwyll meets and marries Rhiannon   col. 12.27-27.8
                                         14½ col.
3. Pryderi's birth, disappearance and return   col. 27.8-38.11
                                         11 col.

The Second Branch
Branwen has but two obvious sections:
1. Matholwch in Wales   col. 38.12-48.6
                                         10 col.
2. Troubles in Ireland; return with Brân's head   col. 48.6-61.19
                                         13¼ col.

The Third Branch
Manawydan, too, has two sections:
1. The tale of the four friends   col. 61.20-71.15
                                         10 col.
2. The tale of Manawydan and Cigfa   col. 71.15-81.19
                                         10.col.

The Fourth Branch
In *Math* the tripartite structure returns:
1. Gwydion and Gilfaethwy's treason and   col. 81.20-92.4
   punishment   11½ col.

2. Aranrhod's three curses	col. 92.4-101.17
	8½ col.
3. Blodeuwedd's treachery	col. 101.17-111.16
	10. col.

Each section, or episode, of each branch seems to average 10-11 columns of *Llyfr Gwyn Rhydderch*; indeed, if the text were to be read aloud the discrepancy between the episodes might prove to be even less, because some parts of the narrative flow more quickly than others. There are at least four possible reasons for this symmetry: it may be a pure coincidence, due to the way I have preferred to divide the tales [compare, for example, R.M. Jones' divisions, 1983]; the author may have adapted the length of the narrative because of the limitations imposed on him by the size of his manuscript; the symmetry may reflect an attempt to create sections suitable for public readings of the written text [James 1991:37]; or the author may have been strongly influenced by the oral performance of *Pedeir Keinc y Mabinogi,* in which symmetrical composition may have played an important part. If we accept the last interpretation, then the oral performance has influenced the branches to a greater degree than previouly considered.

This raises an important question when considering the performance of the tales. Were the tales narrated in sections rather than as a complete whole? This is common practice in other countries, and therefore why not in Wales [Clover 1986]? This would be one explanation for the episodic structure so apparent in the *Pedeir Keinc.* Each episode is independent, to a large degree, and it is possible to analyse each one independently. Of course, as already emphasised, such a structure is characteristic of an oral tale—a chronological, episodic, simple structure—that does not make too many demands on the memory of the performer.

Tripartite Structure

One feature that becomes apparent when analysing the structure of *Pedeir Keinc y Mabinogi,* and the tales of the *Mabinogion* in general, is the extensive use of the triad. Since the earliest records it is apparent that the Celts favoured classifying in threes. According to Axel Olrik [1965:133], this is one of the principal laws governing the composition of folk narrative:

24

> Nothing distinguishes the great bulk of folk narrative from modern
> literature and from reality as much as does the number three. Such a
> ruthlessly rigid structuring of life stands apart from all else.

This is relevant to the structure of the *Pedeir Keinc*. *Pwyll* contains the tale of Arawn, Rhiannon and Pryderi. There are three sections in *Math,* relating the treachery of Gwydion and Gilfaethwy, the three curses of Aranrhod and the infidelity of Blodeuwedd. Two of the four branches therefore have a tripartite structure. Surely it was easier to commit a tale to memory if it was composed of a certain number of sections—the storyteller had merely to recall the titles of each section, and he would then remember the content. The extant *Trioedd Ynys Prydein* (The Triads of the Island of Britain) are, of course, proof of an early practice whereby the storytellers and poets catalogued early Welsh traditions in triadic patterns [Bromwich 1978]. The earliest texts go back to the thirteenth century and are in essence a catalogue of the names of traditional heroes and events, grouped in threes. At the end of *Branwen* we are given a summary of the entire content of the branch:

1. o achaws Paluawt Branwen
2. ac o achaws Yspadawt Uran
3. ac am y ginyaw yn Hardlech
   ac am Ganyat adar Riannon
   ac am Yspydaut Benn.
(1. concerning the Blow to Branwen
2. and concerning the feast of Bran
3. and concerning the feast in Hardlech
   and concerning the song of the birds of Rhiannon
   and concerning the feast of the Head.)

The numbers and divisions above are my own. It is unclear why the author should choose to give a summary here, but not at the end of the other branches. There may have existed summaries for each tale, which were thoroughly memorized by the storyteller, so that he should not forget any part of the tale. Such summaries would have to be easy to memorize—some feature would have to link together each section title. In the summary of *Branwen,* there exists an interlace of the section titles with various sound correspondences: Paluawt— Yspadawt—Yspydawt—cinyaw—canyat. It is impossible to say whether this tale summary is an addition on the part of the scribe, or whether it is a direct reflection of the craft of the storyteller—whether it is a conscious effort on the scribe's part to draw together all the separate episodes, or whether it was part of the narrator's technique to try and memorize the essential components of the story. The author here actually gives five titles, although the last three—all beginning with *ac am* (and concerning) (a triad within a triad)—could be combined into the third section of the tale. W.J. Gruffydd maintains that these sub-titles refer to different components of the story, which the author of *Branwen* brought together for the first time [1953:6-10]. His argument is that there is a lack of unity in the text of *Branwen* compared with the other branches, and that the latter contain no sub-titles. Mac Cana, however, shows that it was a fairly common practice to insert sub-titles in Irish literature. He shows how the author of *Fled Bricrenn* does this and suggests that the practice may have influenced the author of *Branwen* [1958:140-150].

All this suggests that tale summaries may well have been used by oral tellers, and that most stories were divided into sections—perhaps into three—the titles of which would be memorised by the redactor. Since the triads were a popular means of recording the names of traditional characters, it is reasonable to suppose that triads were created to record the contents of particular tales and that this is why many of the eleven tales of the *Mabinogion* divide themselves so readily into three parts.

Tripartite structure is also important within individual episodes in the tales. Emphasis in written literature can be obtained by the degree and detail of the description of an object or event. However, folk narrative lacks this detail, and its spare descriptions are too brief to serve as a means of emphasis. For the traditional oral narrative the only alternative, according to Axel Olrik, is repetition [1965:132-133; Gray 1971]. This builds up tension and also fills out the body of the narrative. Moreover, this repetition is almost always tied to the number three. Note the following examples in the *Pedeir Keinc*:

Pwyll	Pwyll sees Rhiannon on three consecutive days
Branwen	Efnysien asks three times, 'Beth yssyd yn y boly hwnn?' ('What is in this sack?') and the answer is the same each time. Efnysien then crushes the skull of the soldier in the sack. After killing two soldiers, the narrator uses a summarising technique to avoid further repetition: 'Sef a wnai ynteu yr un guare a fawb ohonunt . . .' ('He played the same way with each of them . . .'). Thus, although Efnysien actually kills two hundred men, the act itself is only described three times.

26

Manawydan	The four friends stay in England for a time and are confronted with three parallel situations.
	Manawydan sows his seeds in three separate fields, and the narrator relates what happens in each field.
	Manawydan makes three attempts at hanging the mouse.
Math	Gwydion and Gilfaethwy are three times transformed into animals.
	Aranrhod swears three destinies upon her son, which give rise to three parallel situations.
	Gronw Pebyr asks for leave of absence three times.

In most cases the narrator builds up to a climax on the third occasion. He usually describes the first scene in full, but uses a summarising technique for the second and third so that every detail is not retold. The same phrases and words are often repeated, but within a different sentence pattern so that although the passage may sound familiar to the audience, listeners are not bored by exact repetition.

Repetition is also employed for another purpose in an oral tale, that which is described by Walter Ong as 'redundancy, repetition of the just-said' [1982:39-41]. When reading a book it is possible to look back over the text if any complication or misunderstanding were to arise, but when listening to an oral performance the listener is given only one chance. However, very often repetition is employed to ensure that the listener is clear in his mind and understands the tale. A good example of this is found in *Branwen* when Brân gives instructions to the seven survivors who then follow his instructions carefully. Similar examples are to be found in *Pwyll*—Arawn gives instructions to Pwyll and Pwyll follows them; Rhiannon explains to Pwyll how to win her hand and Pwyll acts according to her instructions. This is a technique that appears perhaps laborious to us today, but that was all important in the context of an oral performance.

Conclusion

Pedeir Keinc y Mabinogi therefore have a chronological, episodic structure, and a single thread to the narrative. Perhaps episodes were narrated independently, and it could be that the length of the episodes bears a relationship to the original oral performance. As Roger Middleton says [1976:148]:

> in a society where the story-teller's art flourishes even those productions which are given a written form, but intended for public performance, will be affected by the style characteristics of improvisation.

The storytellers' performances will have influenced the author's idea of how to narrate a tale, and the audience would still expect a presentation in the traditional mode.

3 NARRATIVE TECHNIQUES

The importance of the oral tradition in any discussion of *Pedeir Keinc y Mabinogi* has already been noted, and when turning our attention to the stylistic features of the branches we see that this is an essential consideration. The tales belong in essence to the oral tradition, and the influences of that tradition are to be seen clearly on their style [Davies 1993]. We have no direct evidence regarding the techniques or style of the medieval Welsh storytellers when narrating their tales orally. But it is possible to come to some general conclusions regarding the narrative techniques and methods of oral storytellers by studying folk tales collected in Celtic and other countries. By examining such collections we can argue that the style of *Pedeir Keinc y Mabinogi* in their written form owes much to the craft of the *cyfarwydd*. The expression was tempered when the tales were transmitted to a written form, but the implication is that the author recognised and respected the same conventions when narrating a tale, conventions that were originally part of the oral performance of the *cyfarwydd*.

Chronological order and additive style

The main purpose of the medieval storyteller was to entertain, as testified by Gwydion in the fourth branch:

> A'r nos honno, didanu y llys a wnaeth ar ymdidaneu digrif a chyuarwydyt, yny oed hoff gan paub o'r llys, ac yn didan gan Pryderi ymdidan ac ef. [p.69]
> (And that night he entertained the court with pleasant tales and storytelling till he was praised by everyone in the court, and it was a pleasure for Pryderi to converse with him.) [p.57]

A storyteller would entertain his audience by causing them to see a sequence of strange events. The medieval audience was on the whole illiterate—listeners would not expect a tale making great intellectual demands. Therefore we find the narrator moving suddenly from one event to the next without pausing for explanation. As W.L. Evans says when discussing some narrative techniques in medieval Welsh literature [1960:156]:

> An audience of a spoken tale has a primitive feeling for an ordered narrative, and the unity of time is therefore seldom violated.

29

We have already seen that the tales have a clear chronological structure. All events belong to the past, and this leads us to an important feature in the craft of the storyteller. The narrator was expected to cover the transition from one period to the next—the interstices between the important and exciting occasions had to be filled. The art of linking major events was an important part of the narrator's craft and is seen in passages such as:

Pwyll Y'r llys y doethant, a threulaw y nos honno a orugant drwy gerdeu a chyuedach, ual y bu llonyd ganthunt. A thrannoeth diuyrru y dyd a wnaethant yny oed amser mynent y wwyta. [p. 11]
(They came to the court, and they spent that night in song and carousal, so that they were well content. And on the morrow they spent the day until it was time to go to eat.) [p.11]

Branwen Dilit ymdidan a wnaethant y nos honno, tra uu da ganthunt, a cherd a chyuedach. A phan welsant uot yn llessach udunt uynet y gyscu noc eisted a wei hwy, y gyscu yd aethant. [p.37]
(They continued to converse that night, while it pleased them, and to carouse. And when they realised that it was better for them to go to sleep than to sit any longer, they went to sleep.) [p.26]

The effect of this emphasis on progression is noticeable on *Pedeir Keinc y Mabinogi*.

A great number of 'connectors' are seen throughout the tales, for example:

> Ac yna; ac ar hynny; a gwedy; a thrannoeth; a'r dyd hwnnw.
> (And then; and upon that; and then; and the following day; and that day.)

Here we see the style of the elementary storyteller, a style that every school child today is taught to avoid when writing [Ong 1982:38; Tannen 1982]. The word *ac* (and) usually links the statements, and the text consists of sequences of simple sentences. Note the following passage from *Pwyll*:

> Ac yna edrych ohonaw ef ar liw yr erchwys, heb hanbwyllaw edrych ar y carw. Ac o'r a welsei ef o helgwn y byt, ny welsei cwn un lliw ac wynt. Sef lliw oed arnunt, claerwyn llathreit, ac eu clusteu yn gochyon. Ac ual y llathrei wynnet y cwn, y llathrei cochet y clusteu. Ac ar hynny at y cwn y doeth ef, a gyrru yr erchwys a ladyssei y carw e ymdeith, a llithyaw y erchwys e hunan ar y carw. Ac ual y byd yn llithiau y cwn, ef a welei uarchauc yn dyuot yn ol yr erchwys y ar uarch erchlas mawr;

a chorn canu am y uynwgyl, a gwisc o urethyn llwyt tei amdanaw yn
wisc hela. Ac ar hynny y marchawc a doeth attaw ef, a dywedut ual
hynn wrthaw... [pp.1-2]
(And then he looked at the colour of the pack, without troubling to look
at the stag. And of all the hounds he had seen in the world, he had seen
no dogs the colour of these. The colour that was on them was a brilliant
shining white, and their ears red. And as the whiteness of the dogs
shone, so shone the redness of their ears. And with that he came to the
dogs, and drove away the pack that had killed the stag, and baited his
own pack upon the stag. And while he was baiting his dogs he could see
a horseman coming after the pack on a big dapple-grey steed, and a
hunting horn round his neck, and a garment of light grey cloth about
him by way of hunting garb. And upon that the horseman drew near
him, and spoke to him thus...) [pp.3-4]

Such a style would hardly be approved in a literary work today. Yet,
if the passage is read aloud, the *ac* (and) does not draw attention to
itself at all—it is an integral part of the composition, leading the
narrative on swiftly and reflecting the sudden movements that
culminate in Pwyll's meeting with Arawn. The author cleverly avoids
a surfeit of verbs in the third person preterite tense—as T.J. Morgan
has shown in his seminal article on the style of medieval Welsh prose,
the author succeeds in varying the sentence syntax [1951:161-175;
Evans 1976]. Let us examine the above passage once again:

Ac yna edrych ohonaw ef   —verb noun + preposition *o* + subject
(And then he looked)

at y cwn y doeth ef   —mixed sentence
(to the dogs he came)

a gyrru yr erchwys   —verb noun
(and sent the pack)

a llithyaw   —verb noun
(and fed)

Ac ual y byd yn llithiau y cwn   —historic present
(And as he is feeding the dogs)

ef a welei   —abnormal sentence
(he saw)

31

y marchawc a doeth attaw ef   —abnormal sentence
(the rider came to him)

a dywedut   —verb noun
(and said)

Further examples of such variation in syntax can be found, for example:

Dyuot deu Wydel uonllwm idaw [p.44]
—verb noun + subject
(Two bare-breeched Irishmen came to him) [p.37]

Kyuodi a orugant pawb o niuer y llys [p.31]
—verb noun + *a* + auxiliary verb
(All the host of the court arose) [p.26]

Ac ar hynny, nachaf un o'r llongeu yn raculaenu rac y rei ereill [p.30]
—exclamation + subject
(And upon that, behold one of the ships proceeding before the others) [p.25]

This seems to have been a device that developed to avoid monotony in narrative prose, a device that originated in the function, craft and performance of the *cyfarwydd*.

The Formula

Another obvious feature of *Pedeir Keinc y Mabinogi* and the tales of the *Mabinogion* generally is the formula. It is certain that the formula in written literature does not have the same importance and function as in an oral performance of the same tale. Yet, the formulaic technique is an integral part of the composition of *Pedeir Keinc y Mabinogi* and deserves close attention in any study of the style of the tales [Davies 1988b]. The meaning of formula in this context is a set of words employed to indicate or describe a certain idea. Much research has been done on the formula and formulaic composition in Homeric verse. One of the most important scholars in this field was Milman Parry—it was he, together with his student Albert Lord, who developed the theory that formulaic composition is synonymous with oral composition [Parry 1971; Lord 1960]. According to Parry, the formula developed as an element in oral composition: in the course of time the need for a particular phrase arises over and over again; the phrase therefore becomes fixed and the poet uses it regularly, under

32

the same metrical conditions, thus creating a formula. The unlettered singer, therefore, builds up a reserve of ready-made formulae which enables him to rise immediately to most needs that his subject forces on him. By comparing Homeric diction with that of the South Slavic heroic songs, Parry concludes that the heroic epics were the product of an oral poetic tradition—they had originally been composed orally. According to Parry's theory, therefore, the main feature of orally composed poetry is its formulaic character, and the recurrence of formulae brands a poem as oral. The use of Parry's methods has been accompanied by increasing questions about the validity of some of his most basic assumptions and definitions, including his definition of a formula [Finnegan 1990]. Also, there is little agreement on whether formulaic style implies oral composition, whether literacy and oral composition are always mutually exclusive. Many believe Parry's definition of the formula to be too narrow [Russo 1976], and that it should embrace more than the fixed noun-epithet combinations of Parry's first study. Indeed, Parry himself emphasises a 'formula-system', introducing the concept of the open variable combined with the fixed element to form a larger unit, and prepares the way for further broadening of the definition by saying that there were still 'more general types of formulas'; not only were there fixed or verbatim formulae, but also fluid formulae that resemble others 'in rhythm, in parts of speech, and in one important word' [Russo 1976:32; Parry 1971:313].

To what extent can these theories be applied to prose, and to medieval Welsh prose in this particular case? Metre is an essential ingredient in the Parry-Lord formula. Even so, there have been many attempts to adapt the theory to prose. Ilhan Basgöz, for example, in his treatment of the *hikaye* of Azerbaijan, argues that verbal repetition is a distinct feature of orally transmitted literature, prose and verse alike [1978:1; Gray 1971]. He defines the prose formula as a traditional, literary unit of verbal repetition which expresses a given essential idea (formula-thought) in one or more phrases [1978:3]. Isidore Okpewho, too, comes to the conclusion that there is nothing particularly metrical about the formula [1977:190]:

> ... the formulary device is simply a case of memory pressed into a pattern of convenience, and is by no means peculiar to a prosodic context ...

33

Kevin O'Nolan applied the formula concept to Irish medieval prose romances and he, too, concludes that metre has no essential connection with formulae [1975; 1978]. Edgar Slotkin, on the other hand, has argued that there is no such thing as an oral prose formula in the sense of formula defined by Parry and Lord—one must be able to show that there is a high density of formulae in a text and that they are necessary to the composition before one can argue for an oral provenance [1991]. Slotkin's paper raises very important issues. However, I would tend to agree with Rosenberg [1981:443], who argues that in almost all applications of the theory to national literatures the starting point has been a modification of the original conception, adjusted to suit the demands of the particular language being studied and the tradition in which it was being performed. There are difficulties in adapting the classical Parry-Lord analyses to prose narratives. Perhaps it would be safer to avoid the term 'formula' with all its connotations, and employ another term such as 'verbal repetition' or 'traditional pattern' when dealing with prose. However, in spite of the possible confusion, I have chosen to use the term 'formula' in my analysis of *Pedeir Keinc y Mabinogi,* although I wish to make it clear that I do not use it in the Parry-Lord sense. Neither do I equate the presence of formulae with oral composition. The four tales under discussion are not markedly formulaic [Roberts 1984: 216], yet I would argue that certain phrases and descriptions are used so frequently that they must be more than chance combinations: we can be fairly certain that we are dealing with an acquired technique. The suggestion is that the author (and the authors of the *Mabinogion* tales in general) was drawing on a stock of stereotyped forms of expression or formulae, and that he would build on these as the need arose. This is not to say that the tales were composed orally; yet the implication is that these formulae were part of the technique of the oral storyteller and that the oral style has left its mark on the written texts.

Linguistic Formulae

Let us first examine the linguistic formulae in the *Pedeir Keinc,* those formulae that are apparent in dialogue passages and were, it would seem, part of the every day language of the period. Although they do not further the development of the plot in any way, they are important as regards the presentation and maintaining of dialogue. Oaths and greetings belong to this category. In the *Pedeir Keinc* two formulae occur in conjunction with each other when greeting, that is one character greets and the other replies at once. *Duw a rodo da yt (a chraessaw duw wrthyt)* (God be good to you (and God's welcome to you)) is the usual answer. The first greeting is *Dyd da itt* (Good day to you), *Henpych guell* (Greetings) or an indirect greeting, that is *cyfarch guell idaw* (greeted him). Here is an example from *Pwyll*:

> a guedy y dyuot y gynted y neuad kyuarch guell a wnaeth y Wawl uab Clut a'y gedymdeithon o wyr a gwraged. 'Duw a ro da yt,' heb y Gwawl, 'a chraessaw Duw wrthyt.' [p.16]
> (and when he came to the upper part of the hall he greeted Gwawl son of Clut and his company of men and women. 'God be good to you,' said Gwawl, 'and God's welcome to you.') [p.15]

Note how the author plays on this formula when describing Pwyll and Arawn's first encounter:

> 'A unben,' heb ef [Arawn], 'mi a wnn pwy wytti, ac ny chyuarchaf i well it.' [p.2]
> ('Ah lord,' he said [Arawn], 'I know who you are, and I will not greet you.') [p.4]

Usually it is the character of lower status who greets first, and the other responds by wishing him *graessaw Duw* (God's welcome) [T.Charles-Edwards 1978]. Pwyll believes Arawn is refusing to greet him because of his status. However, when Pwyll realises that Arawn is a king, and therefore of higher rank, he responds immediately:

> 'Arglwyd,' heb ynteu, 'dyd da itt...' [p.2]
> ('Lord,' he said, 'good day to you...') [p.4]

This is an interesting example, therefore, of using a formula for a specific purpose.

Many types of oaths are found in the text:

Y rof i a Duw (Between me and God)
Dioer (God knows)
Yr Duw (For God's sake)
Ym kyffes i Duw; I Duw y dygaf uyg kyffes; dygaf y duw uyg kyffes
(By my confession to God; to God I bear my confession; I bear to God my confession)
Meuyl ar uy maryf; mefl (Shame on my beard; shame)
Oy a arglwyd Duw; Oy a uab Duw; Oy a Duw holl gyuoethawc; Oy a Duw
(Oh lord God; Oh son of God; Oh all powerful God; Oh God)

A detailed analysis of the oaths in the *Mabinogion* corpus points to the existence of some sort of system—they have a particular location within the speech, various oaths occur under the same grammatical conditions (e.g. after a negative), and most oaths are followed by a speech marker (e.g. he/she said).

Variable Formulae

The oaths are verbatim formulae; the greetings are combinations of verbatim units which unite to give a longer formula. Although the verbatim formulae were an aid to the oral narrator, perhaps the need for them was not so great when the tales were committed to manuscript. This is why we see more variable formulae, where identity is established by similar structural patterns and repetition of key words. Formulae of this type are much more common in the *Pedeir Keinc,* suggesting perhaps that the tales reflect a more developed and more sophisticated mode of expression than that of the oral storyteller.

Variable formulae are used in *Pedeir Keinc y Mabinogi* to describe physical appearance [Davies 1988a]. There are very few long and detailed descriptions in the tales, and very few adjectives, for example:

Pwyll   . . . wynt a welynt yn dyuot y mywn, guas gwineu, mawr, teyrneid, a guisc o bali amdanaw. [p.13]
              (. . . they saw entering a large, princely, auburn-haired youth, and a dress of silk about him.) [p.13]

Branwen A mi a welwn gwr melyngoch mawr yn dyuot or llyn [p.35]
              (And I saw a large ginger-haired man coming from the lake) [p.30]

Most of the descriptions are introduced by the verb *gweld* (to see); the character's personal name is not mentioned; a brief description of the character's dress is sometimes given, following the same pattern in *Pwyll*:

    gwisc o bali amdanaw   (a dress of silk about him)
    gwisc o urethyn . . . amdanaw (a dress of cloth . . . about him)

and reference is made to hair colour without using the noun *gwallt* (hair) at all. Although there are only a few short descriptions in *Pedeir Keinc y Mabinogi,* yet the common elements suggest the existence of a particular convention when describing physical appearance. Indeed, the same type of simple description can be seen throughout the tales of the *Mabinogion*. One feature that becomes apparent is that every description has been structured in a particular way—formulae, or rather short formulaic units, are combined, containing a noun + descriptive element (an adjective/adjectives or *o* [of] + material of dress). These formulaic descriptions found in *Pedeir Keinc y Mabinogi* are therefore examples of a technique that was used extensively. However, the descriptions found in *Pwyll* are much more developed than those found in *Branwen* and *Math,* and not one description of this type is found in *Manawydan*.

Pwyll also stands apart since it is also the only branch to employ a combat formula, although one could argue that the opportunity does not arise to use such a formula in the other three tales. This formula is used extensively in the Three Romances, especially in *Gereint*. There are four combinations to this formula in *Pwyll*:

> Ac ar hynny y deu urenhin a nessayssant y gyt am perued y ryt e ymgyuaruot. Ac ar y gossot kyntaf y gwr a oed yn lle Arawn, a ossodes ar Hafgan ym perued bogel y daryan yny hyllt yn deu hanner, ac yny dyrr yr arueu oll, ac yny uyd Hafgan hyt y ureich a'e paladyr dros pedrein y uarch y'r llawr, ac angheuawl dyrnawt yndaw ynteu. [p.5]
> (And upon that the two kings approached each other towards the middle of the ford for the encounter. And at the first attack the man who was in Arawn's place struck Hafgan on the centre of his shield's boss, so that it was split in two and all his armour broken, and Hafgan was his arm and his spear's length over his horse's crupper to the ground, and a mortal wound upon him.) [p.6]

Here we see the *gossot* (attack), the place of attack, the result of the attack on the enemy's arms, and the result on the enemy himself.

It has already been observed that in oral narrative care is taken to cover the transition from one period to the next—the interstices between the important and exciting occasions are almost always filled. Naturally, formulae are employed for this purpose. When attempting to outline the action from one day to the next, formulaic units are combined in the *Pedeir Keinc*. There are three stages here: *treulaw/dilit* (spend/follow); *cysgu* (sleep); *trannoeth* (the following day). Note two examples:

Pwyll   Bwyta a chyuedach a wnaethont, ac amser a doeth y uynet y gyscu. Ac y'r ystauell yd aeth Pwyll a Riannon, a threulaw y nos honno drwy digriuwch a llonydwch. A thrannoeth yn ieuengtit y dyd. . . [p.18]

37

(They ate and caroused, and time came to go to sleep. And
Pwyll and Rhiannon went to the room, and spent that night in
pleasure and satisfaction. And early the following day...)
[p.16]

Branwen   Dilit y gyuedach a wnaethant ac ymdidan. A phan welsant uot
yn well udunt kymryt hun no dilyt kyuedach, y gyscu yd
aethant. A'r nos honno y kyscwys Matholwch gan Uranwen. A
thrannoeth, kyuodi a orugant pawb o niuer y llys... [p.31]
(They followed the feasting and talked. And when they saw that
it was better to sleep than to follow the carousal, they went to
sleep. And that night Matholwch slept with Branwen. And the
following day, everyone in the court arose...) [p.26]

Sometimes a description precedes the reference to the feast, that is a
description of the welcome, the preparation, and the seating arrange-
ments at table. In this context units are combined yet again to express
(a) the welcome and preparation; (b) sitting at table; (c) the seating
arrangement; (d) the beginning of the feasting. The same basic
structure is found in each example, but the details are varied for each
individual situation, for example:

Branwen   Yn Aberfraw dechreu y wled, ac eisted. Sef ual yd eistedyssant,
brenhin Ynys y Kedeirn, a Manawydan uab Llyr o'r neill parth
idaw, a Matholwch o'r parth arall, a Branwen uerch Lyr gyt ac
ynteu... A'r gyuedach a dechreussant. [p.31]
(In Aberfraw they began the feast, and sat down. This is how
they sat, the king of the Island of the Mighty, and Manawydan
son of Llyr on his one side, and Matholwch on his other, and
Branwen daughter of Llyr with him... And they began the
carousal.) [p.26]

Although the units in this formula are not verbatim, key words are
employed during each stage of events, giving the impression of
familiarity.

Lastly in this category, formulaic units are combined when
describing an approach to a building. Each description is preceded by
the verb *gweld* (to see), that is the listener sees everything through the
eyes of the protagonist. It is interesting to note the use made of
detailing or precise focusing, for example:

Manawydan   A chan y geir hwnnw mynet allan, ac y traws y managassei ef
uot y gwr a'r gaer, kyrchu a wnaeth hitheu. Porth y gaer a
welas yn agoret; ny bu argel arnei. Ac y mywn y doeth, ac y gyt
ac y doeth... [p.57]

38

(And with that word she went out, and in the direction he told her the man and the fort were, she proceeded. She saw the gate of the fort open; it was not concealed. And she came in, and as soon as she came. . .) [p.47]

This is a dramatic device where tension is maintained as the listener moves, one step at at a time, with Rhiannon into the fort. Evans [1960:109, 143-147] refers to this as the observing eye technique, while Roberts [1984:218] compares it to a T.V. camera panning and finally centering on the significant object or person.

Another type of variable formula exists, where a number of formulaic units are not combined to build up the description. Instead there is only one verbal pattern, and a clear structure within that. These variable formulae are therefore much shorter than those already discussed. Three of the four branches begin in the same way, with the name of a lord, the name of his land, and the location of the lord at that particular time. Before the last element there is a 'time' phrase which focuses the attention on a particular event:

Pwyll   Pwyll, Pendeuic Dyuet, a oed yn arglwyd ar seith cantref Dyuet. A threigylgweith yd oed yn Arberth, prif lys idaw. . . [p.1]
(Pwyll, Prince of Dyfed, was lord over the seven commotes of Dyfed. And once upon a time he was in Arberth, a chief court of his. . .) [p.3]

Branwen   Bendigeiduran uab Llyr, a oed urenhin coronawc ar yr ynys hon, ac ardyrchawc o goron Lundein. A frynhawngueith yd oed yn Hardlech yn Ardudwy, yn llys idaw. [p.25]
(Bendigeidfran son of Llyr was crowned king over this island, and exalted with the crown of London. And one afternoon he was in Harlech in Ardudwy, in a court of his.) [p.25]

Math   Math uab Mathonwy oed arglwyd ar Wyned, a Pryderi uab Pwyll oed arglwyd ar un cantref ar ugeint yn y Deheu. . . . dydgweith. . . [p.67]
(Math son of Mathonwy was lord over Gwynedd, and Pryderi son of Pwyll was lord over twenty one commotes in the South. . . one day.) [p.55]

There is no opening formula in the third branch which may imply that *Branwen* and *Manawydan* were *one* branch originally.

A variable formula is often used to open other tales of the *Mabinogion*. For example:

39

Owein   Yr amherawdyr Arthur oed yg Kaer Llion ar Wysc. Sef yd oed
yn eisted diwarnawt yn y ystauell... [Thomson 1968: 1]
(The emperor Arthur was in Caer Llion on Usk. And he was
sitting there one day in his room...) [p.155]

Each branch ends with the same formula:

Pwyll   Ac yuelly y teruyna y geing hon yma o'r Mabynnogyon. [p.27]
(And so ends this branch of the Mabinogion.) [24]
Branwen   A llyna ual y teruyna y geing honn o'r Mabinyogi, o achaws...
[p.48]
(And so ends this branch of the Mabinogi, because of...) [p.40]
Manawydan Ac yuelly y teruyna y geing honn yma o'r Mabinogy. [p.65]
(And so ends this branch of the Mabinogi.) [p.54]
Math   Ac yuelly y teruyna y geing honn o'r Mabinogi. [p.92]
(And so ends this branch of the Mabinogi.) [p.75]

Note that *llyna* occurs in *Branwen,* but *yuelly* in the other branches,
which again may suggest that there was originally no division here
and that the formula at the end of the second branch is a later
addition. In *Manawydan* there is a specific phrase before the formula:

> Ac o achaws y carchar hwnnw y gelwit y kyuarwydyt hwnnw
> Mabinogi Mynweir a Mynord. [p.65]
> (And because of that imprisonment that *cyfarwyddyd* was called
> Mabinogi Mynweir and Mynord.) [p.54]

and this combination of *galw* (to call) + *cyfarwyddyd/chwedl* (tale) is
employed at the end of some of the other tales of the *Mabinogion,* for
example

Owein   A'r chwedyl hwn a elwir Chwedyl Iarlles y Ffynnawn.
[Thomson 1968: 30]
(And this tale is called the Tale of the Lady of the Fountain.)
[p.182]

When using degrees of the adjective to describe people and places,
the narrator again relies on short formulae with a fixed pattern but
with variety in the vocabulary. Two categories can be observed
here—one uses the comparative degree of the adjective and the other
the superlative degree, for example:

Manawydan Mi a debygaf na werendeweist eiryoet ar ymdidanwreic well no
hi. [p.50]
(I am sure that you have never listened to a better
conversationalist than she.) [p.41]

Pwyll   Ac a rodaf y wreic deccaf a weleist eiroet y gyscu gyt a thi
beunoeth. [p.3]
(And I will give the most beautiful woman to sleep with you each
night.) [p.4]

A variable formula is employed to describe the taking of counsel:

Branwen   Yny lle trannoeth kymryt kynghor. Sef a gahat yny kynghor
... [p.30]
(In that place the following day counsel was taken. And he was
advised to...) [p.26]

and also when the need arises to describe a journey. The latter is a
very short formula and contains no details. Yet it emphasises the
importance of accounting for every interstice:

Manawydan Byhyt bynnac y buant ar y fford, wynt a doethant y Dyuet.
[p.55]
(And however long they were on the road, they came to Dyfed.)
[p.45]

By adhering to the same structure in his formulae the storyteller can
maintain the pattern without repeating the same vocabulary. He can
therefore have variation but at the same time he has a basic pattern
which is a continuous help when composing his tale.

The Doublet
The third type of formula seen in *Pedeir Keinc y Mabinogi* and in the
Mabinogion tales in general is the doublet, a combination of two words
which are to all intents synonymous and very often bound together by
alliteration. Some doublets in the *Pedeir Keinc* also occur in other tales
of the *Mabinogion,* for example *y gyuoeth ac y wlat* (his land and country);
am dir a dayar (for land and earth); *hud a lledrith* (magic and enchantment). Without recurrence there is no indication that a doublet is part
of a system which the tradition has established as useful to itself. Yet
one surely cannot ignore the numerous doublets that occur only once
in the *Mabinogion.* Even if one cannot prove that they are part of the
traditional 'system', in all probability they do reflect an attempt on
the part of the narrators to adapt traditional techniques to suit their
favoured mode of expression. Here are a few examples from the *Pedeir
Keinc*:

llys ar kyuanned [p.4]   (court and dwelling) [p.5]
digrifwch a didanwch [p.23]   (pleasure and mirth) [p.20]

41

| car a chedymeith [p.47] | (friend and companion) [p.40] |
| dicter a llit [p.60] | (anger and wrath) [p.50] |

It has been observed that triplets and even foursomes occur in Homer and also in Irish tales, although not often [O'Nolan 1978]. This is found to be the case in Welsh too—a few cases of triplets are found in the *Pedeir Keinc*:

tir a dayar a chyuoeth [p.16]
(land and territory and dominions) [p.15]

o bryt a thwf a meint [p.81]
(in feature, growth and stature) [p.66]

y llongeu ar yscraffeu ar corygeu [p.38]
(the ships and ferry-boats and coracles) [p.32]

By examining the evidence in *Pedeir Keinc y Mabinogi* it would seem that certain phrases and descriptions are used so frequently that they must be more than chance combinations. It is apparent that the author is drawing on a reserve of traditional patterns or formulae that were known to him, and that he built on them and varied them depending on the circumstance. We can be fairly certain therefore that we are dealing with an acquired technique, a technique that can be described as formulaic, and which can be seen to some extent throughout the tales of the *Mabinogion*. This is not to claim that the tales were composed orally and then transmitted to vellum, but rather that the conventions of the oral storytellers have greatly influenced the authors of the written tales, and that the craft of the oral performer has left its mark on their work.

Dialogue

Another important feature when discussing the style of *Pedeir Keinc y Mabinogi* is the use made of dialogue, a technique which again has its origins in the oral tradition [Delargy 1945:33; Bruford 1969]. In the Middle Ages oral entertainment was the prime means of entertainment, and conversation must therefore have been all-important. The ability to hold a conversation was a great virtue:

Pwyll   Ac o'r a welsei eiryoet wrth ymdidan a hi, dissymlaf gwreic a bonedigeidaf i hannwyt a'y hymdidan oed. [p.4]
(And of all he had ever seen, conversing with her, she was the most unaffected woman, and the most gracious of disposition and discourse.) [pp.5-6]

Manawydan Mi a debygaf na werendeweist eiryoet ar ymdidanwreic well no hi. [p.50]
(I am sure that you have never heard a better conversationalist than she.) [p.41]

Conversation would therefore have been a perennial form of entertainment. It remains so today—the interesting conversationalist is a source of entertainment for all. And, indeed, this was the original meaning of the verb *ymddiddan* (to converse)—to entertain each other. What would have been the content of such conversations in the Middle Ages? There would no doubt be news and gossip. But also, surely, anecdotes and humorous occurrences would be related. Teyrnon's conversation is concerned with the *story* of Pryderi's youth:

> Guedy daruot bwyta, ar dechreu kyuedach, ymdidan a wnaethon. Sef ymdidan a uu gan Teirnon, menegi y holl gyfranc am y gassec ac am y mab... [pp.25-26]
> (Having finished eating, at the beginning of the carousal, they conversed. Teyrnon's conversation was to tell the whole story about the mare and about the boy...) [p.22]

Matholwch relates a story as he is conversing:

> A chymeint ac a wnn, mi a'e managaf y ti. Yn hela yd oedwn... [p.35]
> (As much as I know, I will tell you. I was hunting...) [p.30]

and tells Brân the tale of the iron house. Indeed, so often did people relate anecdotes and tales to each other, that *ymddiddan* became a term for a tale, as the romance of *Iarlles y Ffynnawn* (The Lady of the Fountain) suggests:

> 'Weithon,' heb y Kei, 'chwitheu bieu talu y minneu uy ymdidan.'
> 'Kynon,' heb yr Owein, 'tal y ymdidan y Gei.' 'Dioer,' heb y Kynon, 'hyn gwr wyt a gwell ymdidanwr no mi, a mwy a weleist o betheu odidawc; tal di y ymdidan y Gei!' 'Dechreu di,' heb yr Owein, 'o'r hynn odidockaf a wypych.' [Thomson 1968:2]
> ('Now', said Cei, 'it is for you to pay me my story (*ymddiddan*).'
> 'Cynon', said Owein, 'pay Cei his story (*ymddiddan*).' 'God knows,' said Cynon, 'an older man and a better teller of tales (*ymddiddanwr*) are you than I. More have you seen of wondrous things. You pay Cei his tale (*ymddiddan*).' 'You start,' said Owein, 'with the most wondrous thing you know.') [pp.155-156]

An *ymddiddan,* like a *cyfarwyddyd,* is to be full of *petheu odidawc* (wondrous things). There is one main difference, however, between the two narrative forms. In his *ymddiddan,* Cynon talks in the first person; throughout he makes remarks to Cei, and although they elicit no response, Cei is still the chief auditor:

> A hyn a dywedaf ytti, Gei, vot yn debic genhyf . . . [Thomson 1968:3]
> [And I tell you this, Cei, that I am sure . . .) [p.157]

Thus the tale is an *ymddiddan* (= conversation) in so far as Cynon addresses another character, and also speaks in the first person. In a *cyfarwyddyd,* however, the narrator is totally divorced from the tale— he himself took no part in the action of the story. A *cyfarwydd* (storyteller), of course, could also tell *ymddiddaneu:*

> Ynteu Wydyon goreu kyuarwyd yn y byt oed. A'r nos honno, didanu y llys a wnaeth ar ymdidaneu digrif a chyuarwydyt . . . [p.69]
> (He Gwydion was the best storyteller in the world. And that night he entertained the court with pleasant *ymddiddanion* (tales) and *cyfarwyddyd* (storytelling) . . .) [p.57]

It would seem that an *ymddiddan* was a short anecdote recited by a speaker, probably concerning his or her own experiences. But in his performance, a storyteller could also make use of *ymddiddan* in its original sense: he could re-create conversations and dialogue in order to vary his rendering and to create a dramatic atmosphere.

In written literature, the difference between dialogue and narrative can be conveyed by visual devices, but oral storytellers have to rely on the virtuosity of their oral performance, making use of voice, intonation and gesture. One characteristic of the *Four Branches* is the constant use of identification tags or speech markers in passages of dialogue—*heb ef/heb hi* (he said/she said) is the most common. Sometimes the narrator states who is going to speak and to whom; then the speech occurs within which another speech marker, usually involving a pronoun, is embedded:

> Ac ar hynny y marchawc a doeth attaw ef, a dywedut ual hynn wrthaw, 'A unben,' heb ef, 'mi a wnn. . .' [p.2]
> (The horseman drew near him, and spoke to him thus, 'Chieftain,' he said, 'I know. . . [p.4]

This technique is very common in contemporary oral storytelling [Slotkin 1991]—recordings from the Welsh Folk Museum archive prove this beyond any doubt. Alan Bruford [1969:34] attempts to explain the feature in his discussion of dialogue in Irish Romances:

44

It may seem unduly full of apostrophes to the hearer and asservations by the speaker's word, but this again is required by oral delivery. If the speaker begins '*A Chonaill*...' the audience realizes at once that he is speaking to Conall; they might have forgotten who was present at this stage.

Rarely is the embedded marker omitted, as reflected in the following passage:

'Pa achaws,' heb ynteu, 'na dywedy di wrthyf i?' 'Dywedaf wrthyt,' heb hi, 'na dywedeis ys blwydyn y gymmeint yn y kyfryw le a hwnn.' 'Paham?' heb ef. 'Ys glut a beth yd ymdidanyssam ni.' 'Meuyl im,' heb hi, 'yr blwydyn y neithwyr o'r pan elem yn nyblyc yn dillat guely, na digrifwch, nac ymdidan, nac ymchwelut ohonot dy wyneb attaf i, yn chwaethach a uei uwy no hynny o'r bu y rom ni.' Ac yna y medylywys ef. 'Oy a Arglwyd Duw,' heb ef, 'cadarn a ungwr y gydymdeithas, a diffleeis, a geueis i yn gedymdeith.' Ac yna y dywot ef wrth y wreic, 'Arglwydes,' heb ef, 'na chapla di uiui. Y rof i a Duw,' heb ynteu, 'ni chyskeis inheu gyt a thi, yr blwydyn y neithwyr, ac ni orwedeis.' [p.7]
('Why,' he said, 'do you not speak to me?' 'I tell you,' she said, 'for a year I have not spoken so much in such a place as this.' 'Why?' he said. 'We have talked closely together.' 'Shame on me,' she said, 'if since a year from last night, from the time we were enfolded in the bedclothes, there has been neither pleasure nor conversation between us, nor have you turned you face towards me, let alone anything more than that.' And then he thought, 'Oh Lord God,' he said, 'a man steadfast and unswerving of his friendship did I find for a friend.' And then he said to his wife. 'Lady,' he said, 'do not blame me. Between me and God,' he said, 'I have neither slept nor lain down with you since a year from last night.') [p.8]

There are very few passages of dialogue without identification tags in the *Pedeir Keinc*. Here is one example:

Val y byd ynteu yn dodi y dulath yn y fyrch, nachaf offeirat yn dyuot attaw, ar uarch yn gyweir. 'Arglwyd, dyd da it,' heb ef. 'Duw a ro da it,' heb y Manawydan, 'a'th uendith.' 'Bendith Duw it. A pha ryw weith, Arglwyd, yd wyd yn y wneuthur?' 'Crogi lleidyr a geueis yn lledratta arnaf,' heb ef. 'Pa ryw leidyr, Arglwyd?' heb ef. 'Pryf,' heb ynteu 'ar ansawd llygoden...' 'Arglwyd, rac dy welet yn ymodi y pryf hwnnw, mi a'y prynaf. Ellwng ef.' 'Y Duw y dygaf uyghyffes, na'y werthu, na'y ollwng nas gwnaf i.' 'Guir yw, Arglwyd, nyt guerth arnaw ef dim. Rac dy welet ti yn ymhalogi wrth y pryf hwnnw, mi a rodaf it deir punt, a gollwng ef e ymdeith.' 'Na uynhaf, y rof a Duw,'

45

heb ynteu, 'un guerth, namyn yr hwnn a dyly, y grogi.' 'En llawen, Arglwyd, gwna dy uympwy.' E ymdeith yd aeth yr offeirat. Sef a wnaeth ynteu, maglu y llinin am uynwgyl y llygoden. [pp.62-63] (As he was fixing the crossbeam upon the forks, lo, a priest coming towards him on a caparisoned horse. 'Lord, good day to you,' he said. 'God be good to you,' said Manawydan, 'and your blessing.' 'God's blessing on you. And what kind of work are you doing, lord?' 'Hanging a thief whom I caught stealing from me,' he said. 'What kind of a thief, lord?' he said. 'A creature,' he said, 'in the shape of a mouse...' 'Lord, rather than see you handling that creature, I will buy it. Let it go.' 'By my confession to God, I will neither sell it or let it go.' 'The truth is, lord, it has no price set upon it. Rather than see you defiling yourself with that creature I will give you three pounds, and let it go.' 'Between me and God,' he said, 'I want no price for it, save what is its due: to hang it.' 'Gladly, lord, do as you wish.' The priest went away. This is what he did, he noosed the string about the neck of the mouse.) [pp.51-52]

Close analysis of the above passage reveals some very interesting points. Firstly, note how the whole scene is contained within a framework—the steps taken while attempting to hang the mouse. The passage opens in a dramatic manner with the use of the present tense and the exclamation *nachaf* (lo, behold). Then the normal greeting formula is used, and the author establishes immediately the identity of the two speakers. It is interesting to note that the *offeirat* (the priest) greets Manawydan as *arglwydd* (lord) from the very beginning, and the author makes use of this term each time in the ensuing dialogue. The dialogue opens, as one would expect, with the use of speech markers, but then they are omitted. Why should the author choose to deviate from the 'norm'? I would argue that he wishes to speed the rhythm of the dialogue and reflect the pace of the question and answer format between Manawydan and the priest, a feature again found in oral narrative. Both men utter short, simple sentences, and no ambiguity arises regarding the identity of the speaker. And here we realise the significance of the word *arglwydd* (lord). Firstly, the priest wishes to appeal consistently to Manawydan's noble status. But secondly, because of the absence of traditional identification tags, the author uses the word *arglwydd* (lord) to show that the priest is the speaker—after all, the pattern was established in the very first word uttered by him. So the author has ensured that there will be no ambiguity, and at the same time avoids slowing the tempo by means of tags. This serves as an excellent example of how important it is to be conscious of the narrative techniques employed in *Pedeir Keinc y Mabinogi*. By being aware of the 'norm', attention is drawn immediately to the abnormal, so enhancing our reading of the text.

Before proceeding with the general discussion, I should like to place the passage discussed in its context, in order to appreciate further the author's attention to detail when constructing dialogue. This section of *Manawydan* has a tripartite structure—three attempts by Manawydan to hang the mouse and three visitors attempting to foil him—the scholar, the priest and the bishop. Manawydan's first step is to plant 'two forks on the highest place of the mound' [p.50]. Then, use is made of the historic present and an interjection:

> Ac ual y byd yuelly, llyma y guelei... [p.61]
> (And while he is doing this, lo he could see...) [p.50]

Manawydan is greeted in the traditional manner, and note that the term used to greet him is *arglwydd* (lord). The scholar uses this term each time when talking to Manawydan, but here identification tags appear throughout the dialogue, unlike the second passage discussed above. One could argue, therefore, that the only function of *arglwydd* (lord) in the first section is to appeal to Manawydan's status. The third section opens in a dramatic manner yet again. The historic present is not used, but an interjection appears:

> Ac ual yd oed yn y dyrchauael, llyma rwtter escob... [p.63]
> (And as he was raising her, lo a bishop's retinue...) [p.52]

Since Manawydan is in the middle of raising the poor mouse, the dialogue cannot begin immediately as in the two previous cases, and we have a sentence full of tension:

> Sef a wnaeth ynteu, gohir ar y weith. [p.63]
> (What he did was to delay the work.) [p.52]

This time Manawydan realises that it is he who is of lower rank, and must therefore be the first to offer his greeting:

> 'Arglwyd escop,' heb ef, 'dy uendith.' [p.63]
> ('Lord bishop,' he said, 'your blessing.') [p.63]

It is he who greets the stranger as 'lord' on this occasion, suggesting, therefore, that events will be different this time. Upon examining the dialogue, we see that the author uses the traditional tags *heb ef/ynteu* (he said) at the beginning, and then omits them:

'Na uynhaf, y rof a Duw,' heb ynteu. 'Cany mynny hynny, gwna y
guerth.' 'Gwnaf,' heb ynteu, 'rydhau Riannon a Phryderi.' 'Ti a
gehy hynny.' 'Na uynhaf, y rof a Duw.' 'Beth a uynhy ditheu?'
'Guaret yr hut a'r lledrith y ar seith cantref Dyuet.' 'Ti a geffy hynny
heuyt, a gellwng y llygoden.' 'Na ellyngaf, y rof a Duw,' heb ef.
'Gwybot a uynhaf pwy yw y llygoden.' 'Wy gwreic i yw hi, a phy ny
bei hynny nys dillyngwn.' 'Pa gyffuryf y doeth hi attaf i?' 'Y herwa,'
heb ynteu. 'Miui yw Llwyt uab Kil Coet...' [pp.63-64]
('I will not, between me and God,' he said. 'Since you will not have
that, name its price.' 'I will,' he said, 'that Riannon and Pryderi be
set free.' 'You shall have that.' 'I will not, between me and God.'
'What do you want?' 'That the magic and enchantment be removed
from the seven cantrefs of Dyfed.' 'You shall have that also, and let the
mouse go.' 'I will not let it go, between me and God,' he said. 'I want
to know who the mouse is.' 'She is my wife, and were that not so, I
should not free her.' 'How did she come to me?' 'Stealing,' he said. 'I
am Llwyd son of Cil Coed...') [pp.52-53]

As in the second section of the episode, the tempo moves faster, and
because of the nature of the question and answer, no ambiguity arises
regarding identity of speaker. A close examination of this episode,
therefore, highlights the storyteller's art when composing dialogue.
He succeeds in varying the pattern each time—both traditional tags
and *arglwydd* in the first section; traditional tags or *arglwydd* in the
second section; traditional tags and speech with no tags at all in the
final section. This episode began with Cigfa's words:

'A gwna ditheu yn llawen,' heb hi. [p.61]
(And do so gladly,' she said.) [p.50]

Later the priest says:

'En llawen, Arglwyd, gwna dy uympwy.' [p.63]
('Gladly, Lord, do as you wish.') [p.52]

—the same message, but a different syntax. The true gladness is only
revealed the third time, when Manawydan himself says:

'Ellynghaf yn llawen,' heb ef. [p.65]
('I will free her gladly,' he said.) [p.54]

He would not have been happy hanging the mouse—it would have
been a vindictive gesture. True happiness comes from knowing that
the land is peacefully restored to its former glory.
It is clear that dialogue plays an essential part in *Pedeir Keinc y*

Mabinogi. This is reflected in the percentage of direct speech in the narrative:

Pwyll	42% direct speech
Branwen	39% direct speech
Manawydan	43% direct speech
Math	37% direct speech
Overall	40% direct speech

Dialogue is very prevalent in *Pwyll.* The tale progresses by means of dialogue; if the narrative were to be omitted, then there would remain a series of prose dialogues, not unlike the series of saga englynion known as *Canu Llywarch Hen.* The dialogue passages in *Pwyll* are also quite long, so that the author is able to develop the conversation and characters. Turning to *Branwen,* we find that the nature of dialogue is completely different. In this branch there are several long monologues, and the dialogues are generally quite short. The majority are conversations between one character and a group of people, the group speaking as one man, for example Matholwch and his men, Brân and Matholwch's messengers, Efnysien and Brân's men. It would seem that dialogue does not have the same function in *Branwen* as in *Pwyll.* It is more of an ornament in the second branch, and the liveliness and wit seen in *Pwyll* is absent. Turning to *Manawydan,* we see that dialogue is again important. The branch begins with a long conversation between Manawydan and Pryderi; there is a lively conversation between Manawydan and Cigfa, and the passages of conversation at the end of the branch have already been discussed. Here we are back in the realm of the first branch. In *Math* there are few extended passages of dialogue, yet it is an important technique here too. Each major episode contains passages of dialogue, which further the progress of the narrative.

Conclusion

Having examined the evidence offered by the *Four Branches,* I should like to argue that the author has been greatly influenced by the oral storytelling techniques of the medieval *cyfarwydd.* A chronological order and an additive style is characteristic of oral storytellers. Dialogue, too, plays an important part in oral narrative, together with speech markers. I should also like to argue that the author was drawing on a stock of traditional verbal patterns or formulae that were familiar to him, and that these formulae also derive from an oral style.

This is not to say that the tales were composed orally, rather that they have been influenced by the stylistic methods of oral storytellers.

One problem remains, and a study of the style of the branches forces us to face that problem. Most scholars have accepted that the *Pedeir Keinc* are the work of *one* author. But do the stylistic features of the tales confirm this? Are there enough similarities between the formulae, for example, to warrant common authorship? The formula *kymryt kynghor* (to take counsel) is not found in *Pwyll*; the oath *y rof i a duw* (between me and God) does not appear in *Branwen,* although it is very apparent in *Pwyll* and *Manawydan*; the superlative degree of the adjective is used in each case except one in *Pwyll*, while the comparative degree is most obvious in *Manawydan*; only in *Pwyll* and *Branwen* do we have all combinations of the *eistedd wrth y bwrdd* (seating at table) formula; only in *Pwyll* do we find descriptions of dress and of combat; the 'spending time' formula does not occur in *Manawydan*. We have also seen that the function of dialogue varies from branch to branch—it is more prominent in *Pwyll* and *Manawydan* than in *Branwen* and *Math*.

It is clear that there is a relationship between the branches as regards content, and they are unified also by the colophon that occurs at the end of each one. But yet does this necessarily mean that we are dealing with the work of *one* author here? The stylistic features of the branches are similar on the surface, but a closer examination reveals variation in detail. And indeed many of the techniques employed to convey the narrative are common to all tales of the *Mabinogion*. Are the *Pedeir Keinc* therefore a collection of tales composed by men with a common background, respecting the same conventions when narrating a tale, but varying in their use of those conventions? This would be one explanation for the inconsistencies in the *Pedeir Keinc*. It is extremely difficult to answer this question with any certainty, but without doubt it is high time that these branches were looked at anew and the whole question of authorship reconsidered.

4 THEMES

The discussion so far has been mainly concerned with the presentation of the material—the style and structure of the *Pedeir Keinc*. Let us now turn to the material itself. The origins of *Pedeir Keinc y Mabinogi* lie deep in Celtic mythology. It is claimed that the main protagonists were originally gods of Welsh and British tradition—Rhiannon (from *Rigantona, 'Divine Queen'); Teyrnon (from *Tigernonos, 'Divine King'); Lleu, cognate with the Irish Lugh and the continental Lugus [Mac Cana 1983; Green 1986, 1992; Gruffydd 1958]. The family of Dôn corresponds to the Irish Tuatha Dé Danann, and Manawydan to the Irish sea king, Manannán mac Lir. However, as emphasised by Mac Cana [1977:54]:

> the Four Branches... is not a mythological document in any primary sense: it is a literary construct which makes use of mythological, and other, materials. Its author is not a mythographer conscientiously recording the traditions of the gods for their own sake, but a gifted writer shaping the shattered remains of a mythology to his own literary ends.

I do not intend to dwell on the mythological origins of the characters and events in the *Pedeir Keinc,* only emphasise the importance of magic and enchantment throughout the four tales.

The Otherworld and the supernatural

In each branch we see mortals coming into contact with otherworld powers [Gruffydd 1958]. Sometimes the otherworld characters are a help to the hero, sometimes they hinder him. Indeed, this duality is seen very clearly in the portrayal of the Otherworld in *Pedeir Keinc y Mabinogi* [Mac Cana 1983:122-131]. The name given to this magic world in *Pwyll* is Annwfn. In the first branch Arawn is introduced as the king of Annwfn, and Hafgan as another king residing there. Arawn's court is perfection itself:

> Ac yn y llys ef a welei hundyeu ac yneuadeu, ac ysteuyll a'r ardurn teccaf a welsei neb o adeiladeu... Llyma y guelei ef teulu ac yniueroed, a'r niuer hardaf a chyweiraf o'r a welsei neb yn dyuot y mywn, a'r urenhines y gyt ac wynt, yn deccaf gwreic o'r a welsei neb... A threulaw a wnaethant bwyt a llynn a cherdeu a chyuedach.

O'r a welsei o holl lyssoed y dayar, llyna y llys diwallaf o uwyt a llynn, ac eur lestri a theyrn dlysseu. [p.4]
(And in the court he could see sleeping-rooms and halls and chambers and the greatest show of buildings any one had ever seen... Here he could see a war-band and retinues entering, and the most beautiful and smartest troop any one had seen, and the queen with them, the fairest woman any one had ever seen... And they passed the time with food and drink and song and carousal. Of all the courts he had seen on earth, that was the court best furnished with food and drink, and golden vessels and royal jewels.) [p.5]

Note the variation in the formula—rather than the usual *o'r a welsei eiroed* (that he had ever seen) with the superlative degree, the author uses *o'r a welsei o holl lyssoed y dayar* (of all the earthly courts he had seen) which is a subtle reminder to the listener that this is an otherworld court. There is no detailed description here, but an attempt to create an atmosphere of wealth and plenty. The hostile face of the Otherworld is also portrayed, in the person of Hafgan. These two sides are emphasised in the words of one of Pwyll's men as he explains the peculiarity of Gorsedd Arberth (the mound of Arberth):

'Arglwyd,' heb un o'r llys, 'kynnedyf yr orssed yw, pa dylyedauc bynnac a eistedo arnei, nat a odyno heb un o'r deupeth, ay kymriw neu archolleu, neu ynteu a welei rywedawt.' [p.9]
('Lord,' said one of the court, 'it is the peculiarity of the mound that whatever lord sits upon it will not leave it without one of two things, either wounds or blows, or else he will see a wonder.') [p.9]

On that particular occasion, Pwyll saw a wonder; but Manawydan and his companions are not so fortunate in the third branch—they meet with trouble.

We are given a more detailed picture of the Otherworld in *Branwen*, although the word Annwfn is not used. Two otherworld feasts are described as the seven men return with Brân's head to the Island of Britain [G.Jones 1976:194-195]. The first feast is located in Harlech and the second on the island of Gwales. This suggests that there was no specific location to the Otherworld—in the first branch, Annwfn is a country in the middle of Dyfed, with no definite boundaries, and here in the second branch it is a wonderful place by the sea in both instances. The two feasts in the second branch preserve some of the most common characteristics of the Celtic Otherworld. In the feast at Harlech the men are entertained by magic birds, one of the familiar marks of a supernatural realm [Mac Cana 1958:102-107; 1983:124]:

Ac y gyt ac y dechreuyssant wynteu uwyta ac yuet, dyuot tri ederyn, a dechreu canu udunt ryw gerd, ac oc a glywssynt o gerd, diuwyn oed pob un iwrthi hi. A fell dremynt oed udunt y guelet uch benn y weilgi allan. A chyn amlyket oed udunt wy a chyn bydynt gyt ac wy. [p.46] (And as soon as they began to eat and drink, there came three birds and began to sing them a certain song, and of all the songs they had ever heard each one was unlovely compared with that. And they had to look far out over the deep to see them. And they were as clear to them as if they were with them.) [p.39]

According to Brân, these are the birds of Rhiannon, described in the tale of *Culhwch ac Olwen* as 'y rei a duhun y marw ac a huna y byw' (they that wake the dead and lull the living to sleep) [Bromwich and Evans 1992:24; Jones and Jones:115-116].

A Celtic theme, and indeed a common international theme, is reflected in the idea that time does not count in the Otherworld and that everything concerning the mortal world is forgotten [Welsh 1988: 59]. This is the case on the island of Gwales:

Ac yr a welsynt o ouut yn y gwyd, ac yr a gewssynt e hun, ny doy gof udunt wy dim, nac o hynny, nac o alar yn y byt. Aç yno y treulyssant y pedwarugeint mlyned hyt na wybuant wy eiryoet dwyn yspeit digriuach na hyurydach no honno. Nyt oed anesmwythach, nac adnabot o un ar y gilyd y uot yn hynny o amser, no fan doethan yno. [pp.46-47] (And in spite of all the sorrow they had seen before their eyes, and in spite of that they had themselves suffered, they could remember nothing, neither of that or of any sorrow in the world. And there they passed the eighty years so that they knew not of having ever spent a more pleasant and delightful time than that. It was no more uncomfortable than when they came there, nor could any tell by looking at his fellow that it was so long a time.) [p.39]

Very often, if a hero were to return to this world, old age would overcome him, as in the Irish tale of Oisín returning from the Land of Youth. Other times, the magic would disappear on the accomplishing of a prohibited task. On Gwales this involves opening a door:

Ac yny agoroch y drws parth ac Aber Henuelen, y tu ar Gernyw, y gellwch uot yno a'r penn yn dilwgyr genhwch. [p.45] (And until you open the door towards Aber Henfelen, the side facing Cornwall, you can remain there and the head with you uncontaminated.) [p.38]

A similar theme is found in a Welsh folk tale that tells of King Arthur's cave—if the bell is rung in the cave where Arthur and his knights lie sleeping, then Arthur will awake and the cave must be vacated immediately [Rhys 1901:456-497; Gwyndaf 1989:89].

One interesting point arises regarding the Otherworld in *Branwen*, namely the location of the Otherworld. In Ireland, the Otherworld is often an island in the sea, which sometimes disappears in mist. Other times it is a land under the earth, compare the Welsh name—Annwfn —which, according to one explanation, is a combination of *an* (in/inside) and *dwfn* (world) [Williams 1930:99-100]. There are many Welsh folk tales that tell of the fairy folk living underground—they are the children of the *dwfn*. At the turn of the century an interesting tale was recorded by Sir John Rhŷs in his *Celtic Folklore* concerning Plant Rhys Ddwfn (The Children of Rhys Ddwfn), a corruption it would seem of Plant yr Is-Ddwfn (The Children of the Underworld) [Rhŷs 1901:158-161]. According to the tale, these fairy folk inhabited an island off the coast of Dyfed. This is also the location of Gwales— Grassholm island—and it is evident that there are several traditions linking this place with the Otherworld. According to a report about a certain Captain John Evans in the *Pembroke County Guardian* (1896):

> Once when trending up the Channel, and passing Grasholm Island, in what he had always known as deep water, he was surprised to see windward of him a large tract of land covered with a beautiful green meadow. It was not, however, *above water,* but just a few feet *below,* say 2 or 3, so that the grass wavered and swam about as the ripple flowed over it, in a most delightful way to the eye, so that as watched it made one feel quite drowsy. You know, he continued, I have heard old people say there is a floating island off there, that sometimes rises to the surface, or nearly, and then sinks down again fathoms deep, so that no one sees it for years, and when nobody expects it comes up again for a while. How it may be, I do not know, but that is what they say.

And according to Howells' *Cambrian Superstitions* (1831):

> The Milford Haven folk could see the green Fairy Islands distinctly, lying out a short distance from land; and the general belief was that they were densely peopled with fairies. [Rhŷs 1901: 161]

Therefore, over the centuries, the belief has survived that Gwales and its neighbouring islands were places of magic and enchantment, thus linking the Middle Ages with the twentieth century [Loomis 1956: 137-145].

When we turn to *Manawydan* we find an otherworld fort that appears quite unexpectedly in the middle of Dyfed:

> Ac yn ol y baed y kerdassant, yny welynt gaer uawr aruchel, a gueith newyd arnei, yn lle ny welsynt na maen, na gueith eiryoet. [p.55]
> (And they pursued the boar until they could see a huge lofty fort, all newly built, in a place where they had never seen either stone nor building.) [p.46]

Within this fort there are splendid objects which entice Pryderi and his mother. However, this place reflects the harmful side of the Otherworld:

> Ac ar hynny, gyt ac y bu nos, llyma dwrwf arnunt, a chawat o nywl, a chan hynny difflannu y gaer, ac e ymdeith ac wynteu. [p.57]
> (And upon that, as soon as it was night, lo a peal of thunder over them, and a fall of mist, and thereupon the fort vanished, and they disappeared too.) [p.47]

Llwyd the son of Cil Coed employs supernatural powers to imprison Rhiannon and her son in order to avenge the insult done to Gwawl son of Clud in the first branch.

The supernatural is most evident in the fourth branch. There is here no mention of Annwfn as such, yet each episode in this branch deals with characters who possess supernatural powers. Gilfaethwy is able to rape Goewin through magic, and Pryderi is killed 'by dint of strength and valour and by magic and enchantment' [p.60]. Here magic is employed for immoral purposes. But it would seem that magic is justified if used wisely. Math the magician transforms Gwydion and Gilfaethwy into animals as punishment for their misdemeanours. And Gwydion employs his powers to obtain a name, arms and a wife for Lleu in the face of his mother's curse. Lleu is saved from the jaws of death by Gwydion's magic, and at the end of the branch Gwydion is forced to punish his own creation by transforming Blodeuwedd into an owl.

A Moral Code of Conduct

It would seem that the theme of the Otherworld and the continuous fighting against supernatural powers is central to *Pedeir Keinc y Mabinogi*. Very prominent too are themes discussing appropriate moral behaviour [Bollard 1975; Roberts 1980:xviii-xx; Goetinck 1988]. The medieval Welsh law tracts testify that medieval Wales was a period when great emphasis was placed on the nature of insult and shame, the payment of compensation and vengeance [Jenkins 1986]. The themes of *Pedeir Keinc y Mabinogi* reflect clear ideas regarding proper social behaviour.

The First Branch

At the beginning of the first branch Pwyll insults Arawn by feeding the stag to his dogs:

> 'Ny weleis ansyberwyt uwy ar wr,' hep ef, 'no gyrru yr erchwys a ladyssei y carw e ymdeith, a llithiau dy erchwys dy hun arnaw; hynny,' hep ef, 'ansyberwyt oed: a chyn nyt ymdialwyf a thi, y rof i a Duw,' hep ef, 'mi a wnaf o anglot itt guerth can carw.' [p.2]
> ('Greater discourtesy I have not seen in a man,' he said, 'than to drive away the pack that had killed the stag, and to bait your own pack on it; that,' he said, 'was discourtesy, and though I will not take vengeance upon you, between me and God,' he said, 'I will do you dishonour to the value of a hundred stags.') [p.4]

Pwyll pays compensation for the insult by changing places with Arawn and killing Hafgan. The strife between the men is then at an end and a great friendship develops between them. In the second part of the branch Gwawl is insulted twice. Firstly he is insulted when Rhiannon arranges to marry another man although she is promised to Gwawl. He is further insulted when Pwyll tricks him and ties him up in a sack, freeing him on condition 'that he will never lay claim nor seek vengeance for this' [p.16]. Gwawl breaks his word and the vengeance is the theme of the third branch. In the last part of *Pwyll*, Rhiannon suffers insult at the hands of the women who tell untruths about her. Pwyll is determined to adhere to the letter of the law:

> 'Nyt oed achaws ganthunt wy y erchi y mi yscar a'm gwreic namyn na bydei plant idi. Plant a wnn i y uot idi hi. Ac nyt yscaraf a hi. O gwnaeth hitheu gam, kymeret y phenyt amdanaw.' [p.21]
> ('They had no cause to request me to divorce my wife, apart from her having no children. I know she has children, and I will not divorce her. If she has done wrong, let her do penance for it.') [p.19]

She must pay for the wrong she has committed, just as her husband paid for insulting Arawn. We have here an echo of Pwyll's words in the first episode of the tale when he says to Arawn:

> 'A unbenn,' hep ef, 'o gwneuthum gam, mi a brynaf dy gerennyd.' [p.2]

56

('Oh lord,' he said, 'if I have done wrong, I will buy your friendship.')
[p.4]

The irony here, of course, is that Rhiannon is innocent. She attempts to persuade the women to tell the truth, but fails and accepts her punishment stoically. Rhiannon is restored to her rightful place at the end of the branch. No mention is made of the women again—there is no suggestion of vengeance or of punishment. Insult and the payment of compensation are therefore important themes in *Pwyll*.

Attention is also paid to the nature of friendship. Pwyll proves himself to be a faithful friend to Arawn by refusing to sleep with his wife:

'Oy a Arglwyd Duw,' heb ef, 'cadarn a ungwr y gydymdeithas, a diffleeis, a geueis i yn gedymdeith.' [p.7]
('Oh Lord God,' he said, 'a man steadfast and unswerving of his friendship did I find for a friend.') [p.8]

Therefore, in an ironic way, the original insult leads to a lasting friendship between the two characters.

The Second Branch

The nature of insult is a central theme in the second branch, *Branwen*. The first to suffer is Efnysien—his sister Branwen is given as a wife to Matholwch without his permission:

'Ay yuelly y gwnaethant wy am uorwyn kystal a honno, ac yn chwaer y minheu, y rodi heb uyghanyat i? Ny ellynt wy tremic uwy arnaf i,' heb ef. [pp.31-32]
('Is this what they have done with a maiden as excellent as she, and a sister of mine, bestowing her without my consent? They could not insult me more,' he said.) [p.27]

By mutilating Matholwch's horses Efnysien insults the king of Ireland:

'Dioer,' heb ynteu [Matholwch], 'pei ys gwypwn, ny down yma. Cwbyl waradwyd a geueis...' [p.32]
('God knows,' he said [Matholwch], 'had I known, I would not have come here. Full insult have I suffered...') [p.27]

The same word—*tremic* (insult)—is employed to describe the insult done to both Efnysien and Matholwch:

'...A chyt bo gwaradwyd gennyt ti hynny, mwy yw gan Uendigeituran no chenyt ti, y tremic hwnnw a'r guare.' [p.33]
('...And though you reckon that an insult, that insult and trick are more resented by Bendigeidfran than by you.') [p.28]

Bendigeidfran pays compensation for the insult by giving gifts to Matholwch and peace is restored once again. But having returned to Ireland the question of revenge is raised and Matholwch is forced to punish his wife for the insult suffered in Wales. Branwen is sent from her husband's chamber and forced to cook in the kitchen; the butcher comes to her daily and gives her a box on the ear. Bendigeidfran and his men cross over to Ireland to avenge this insult, but Matholwch offers compensation for the injustice:

'Ac y mae Matholwch yn rodi brenhinaeth Iwerdon y Wern uab Matholwch, dy nei ditheu, uab dy chwaer, ac yn y ystynnu y'th wyd di, yn lle y cam a'r codyant a wnaethpwyt y Uranwen...' [p.41]
('And Matholwch is giving the kingship of Ireland to Gwern son of Matholwch, your nephew, your sister's son, and is investing him in your presence, as reparation for the wrong and injustice that have been done to Branwen...') [p.35]

Bendigeidfran is not completely happy with this, and therefore the Irish offer to build him a house too, 'for he never had a house in which he might be contained' [p.35]. But this is not the end of the revenge. The Irishmen plan to hide armed men in the house in order to kill the Welsh, but thanks to Efnysien they are all murdered. It would appear, therefore, that the insult and revenge has finally come to an end:

Ac y doeth gwyr Ynys Iwerdon y'r ty o'r neill parth, a gwyr Ynys y Kedyrn o'r parth arall. Ac yn gynebrwydet ac yd eistedyssant, y bu duundeb y rydunt, ac yd ystynnwyt y urenhinaeth y'r mab. [p.43]
(And the men of the Island of Ireland came into the house on the one side, and the men of the Island of the Mighty on the other. And as soon as they were seated there was concord between them, and the kingship was conferred upon the boy.) [p.36]

But Efnysien has unfinished business—he wants to destroy the boy who is a symbol of the marriage between his sister and the king of Ireland, in other words we have returned to the root of the problem. By throwing the boy into the fire, Efnysien insults the two countries which are now united in the person of Gwern. But Efnysien is a Welshman, and every act of his reflects on his kin. Rather than attack

58

Efnysien as an individual, the Irish set upon all the men of the Island of the Mighty, and a bloody battle ensues. Efnysien realises the outcome of his cruel deed, but it is too late. Ironically, the cauldron given to Matholwch as compensation for Efnysien's original insult is of immeasurable help to the Irishmen. Efnysien destroys it, and in so doing ensures victory to the men of the Island of the Mighty. But it is a futile victory:

> Ac o hynny y bu y meint goruot a uu y wyr Ynys y Kedyrn. Ny bu oruot o hynny eithyr diang seithwyr, a brathu Bendigeiduran yn y troet a guenwynwaew. [p.44]
> (And it was because of that that such victory as there was came to the men of the Island of the Mighty. Even so, there was no victory save for the escape of seven men, and Bendigeidfran was wounded in the foot with a poisoned spear.) [p.37]

This branch emphasises how destructive vengeance can be. Compensation must be paid for insult, but paid once and for all. Efnysien is the catalyst, yet the Irishmen behave no better, in other words evil begets evil. It was suggested at the beginning of the tale that Efnysien was an evil man—destruction and mischief were traits in his character:

> A'r neill o'r gueisson hynny, gwas da oed; ef a barei tangneued y rwg y deu lu, ban uydynt lidyawcaf; sef oed hwnnw Nissyen. Y llall a barei ymlad y rwng y deu uroder, ban uei uwyaf yd ymgerynt. [p.29]
> (And one of those youths was a good youth; he would make peace between the two hosts when they would be most angry; that was Nisien. The other would cause strife between the two brothers when they were most loving.) [p.25]

At the end of this branch one is left wondering what happened to Nisien.

The Third Branch

After the treachery and deceit of the second branch, *Manawydan* makes us realise that there is hope after all. At the beginning of the third branch Manawydan is the character who has suffered injustice, as explained by Pryderi:

> '....Dy geuynderw yssyd urenhin yn Ynys y Kedyrn; a chyn gwnel gameu it,' heb ef, 'ny buost hawlwr tir a dayar eiryoet. Trydyd lledyf unben wyt.' [p.49]

59

('...Your cousin is king in the Island of the Mighty; and though he has done you wrong,' he said, 'you have never been a claimant for land and territory. You are one of the three ungrasping chieftains.') [p.41]

He has reason to seek vengeance—note that the author uses the plural form *cameu* (wrongs) here, rather than the singular noun. But Manawydan is not a man to seek revenge. Friendship—*cydymdeithas*—is all important in this branch, as in the first. Indeed, we are reminded of Arawn's words to Pwyll when Manawydan says to Pryderi:

'Duw a dalo it dy gydymdeithas.' [p.50]
('God repay you your friendship.') [p.41]

and accepts the seven cantrefs of Dyfed together with Rhiannon as a wife. The similarity between the two episodes is further strengthened: upon discovering that Pwyll did not sleep with his wife, Arawn says:

'Oy a Arglwyd Duw,' heb ef, 'cadarn a ungwr y gydymdeithas, a diffleeis, a geueis i yn gedymdeith.' [p.7]
('Oh Lord God,' he said, 'a man steadfast and unswerving of his friendship did I find for a friend.') [p.8]

Compare Manawydan's words:

'...a Duw a dalo y'r gwr yssyd yn rodi i minheu y gedymdeithas mor difleis a hynny.' [p.50]
('...and God repay the man who gives me his friendship as unswerving as that.') [p.42]

The friendship between Manawydan and Rhiannon, Pryderi and Cigfa grows, but an enchantment falls on Dyfed and tests their friendship. Against the advice of Manawydan, Pryderi follows his dogs into a magic fort. Manawydan is accused of being unfaithful to his friend:

'Dioer,' heb y Riannon, 'ys drwc a gedymdeith uuosti, ac ys da a gedymdeith a golleisti.' [pp.56-57]
('God knows,' said Rhiannon, 'a bad friend have you been, and a good friend have you lost.') [p.47]

When Rhiannon and her son disappear, Cigfa too begins to doubt Manawydan; but her brother-in-law shows her the depth of his friendship:

'Dioer,' heb ef, 'cam yd wyt arnaw, os rac uy ouyn i y drygyruerthy di. Mi a rodaf Duw y uach it, na weleisti gedymdeith gywirach noc y keffy di ui, tra uynho Duw it uot uelly. Y rof a Duw, bei et uwni yn dechreu uy ieuengtit, mi a gadwn gywirdeb wrth Pryderi, ac yrot titheu mi a'y cadwn; ac na uit un ouyn arnat,' heb ef. 'E rof a Duw,' heb ef, 'titheu a gey y gedymdeithas a uynych y genhyf i, herwyd uyg gallu i, tra welho Duw yn bot yn y dihirwch hwnn a'r goual.' [p.57] ('God knows,' he said, 'you are mistaken if you are weeping through fear of me. I give you God for surety that you have not seen a friend truer than you will find me, as long as God will that you be this way. Between me and God, were I in the first flush of my youth I would keep faith with Pryderi, and for your sake I would keep it; and let there be no fear upon you,' he said. 'Between me and God,' he said, 'you will have the friendship you desire from me, as far as I can, for as long as it please God that we be in this misery and woe.') [pp.47-48]

We have here an echo of the short episode at the end of the second branch, where Ireland has been laid waste and where 'no person was left alive save five pregnant women' [p.40]. The women give birth to five sons who sleep with each other's mother, thus repopulating the country. In the third branch, however, Manawydan realises that the wasteland situation is not permanent. If we focus in detail on his words above, we see an interesting emphasis placed on God. *Pedeir Keinc y Mabinogi* are set in a non-Christian milieu and it is obvious that the author was conscious of this fact [Bollard 1983: 68]. However, he sometimes fails to keep Christian references out of his text, as shown by Ifor Williams [1930:xxii-xxiv]: the characters swear oaths to God; the spear that wounds Lleu is made during Mass on Sunday; Manawydan is approached by the *yscolheic* (clerk), *offeirat* (priest) and *escob* (bishop) and he asks for their blessing; a name is given to characters at the time of baptism, although the author emphasises that it was 'the baptism that was used then' [p.20,68]. However, in Manawydan's words quoted above there is a veiled suggestion that God is perhaps ultimately responsible for placing the enchantment on Dyfed. Note especially the words 'as long as God will that you be this way' and 'for as long as it please God that we be in this misery and woe'. In the tale of *Culhwch ac Olwen*, God is a character in the story, transforming men into animals because of their sins. In the *Pedeir Keinc*, however, such magical powers are the possession of the magicians Math, Gwydion and Llwyd. But is there a suggestion here that God is testing Manawydan and Cigfa, or at least that it is with God's help that the situation will be resolved? After all, it is through Manawydan's Christian virtues of patience and compromise that the land is restored to its former glory.

61

By the end of the branch we discover that vengeance is at the root of the episode. It is interesting to note how vengeance and friendship are brought together here:

> 'Miui yw Llwyt uab Kil Coet, a mi a dodeis yr hut ar seith cantref Dyuet, ac y dial Guawl uab Clut, *o gedymdeithas ac ef* y dodeis i yr hut . . . ' [p.64]
> ('I am Llwyd son of Cil Coed, and it was I cast the enchantment over the seven cantrefs of Dyfed, and to avenge Gwawl son of Clud, *through friendship for him,* did I cast the enchantment . . . ') [pp. 52-53]

We see here, as in *Branwen,* how vengeance leads to destruction; however, in the third branch Manawydan overcomes treachery and ensures peace once and for all:

> 'Llyna,' heb ef, 'a uynhaf, na bo ymdiala ar Pryderi a Riannon, nac arnaf inheu, uyth am hynn.' [p.64]
> ('This,' he said, 'is what I want, that vengeance never be taken for this upon Pryderi and Rhiannon, nor upon me.') [p.53]

Llwyd gives his word; yet Gwawl had given his word that he would not seek vengeance. The suggestion here, as I see it, is that Gwawl kept his word—he himself did not command the enchantment to be placed on Dyfed. Llwyd acted independently and did so because of his friendship towards Gwawl. After all, Pwyll went too far—it was one thing to tie Gwawl in a sack but to beat and kick him was a great insult. With his clever bargaining Manawydan brings the strife to an end without shedding one drop of blood, surely a lesson to all after the horror and destruction of the second branch.

The Fourth Branch

The opening episodes of *Math* deal once again with the nature of insult. Firstly, Pryderi is insulted as Gwydion tricks him into parting with his pigs. As a result there is fighting and 'great slaughter was made on either hand' [p.59]; there is a return here to the destructive atmosphere of the second branch. But Pryderi does not wish to see utter devastation:

> . . . gyrru kennadeu o Pryderi y erchi guahard y deulu, ac erchi gadu y ryngtaw ef a Guydyon uab Don, canys ef a baryssei hynny . . . 'Dioer,' heb y kennadeu, 'teg, med Pryderi, oed y'r gwr a wnaeth hynn idaw ef o gam, dodi y gorf yn erbyn y eidaw ynteu, a gadu y deu lu yn segur.' [pp.72-73]

(...Pryderi sent messengers to have the two hosts called off, and to ask that it be left to him and Gwydion son of Don, for it was he who had caused that... 'God knows,' said the messengers, 'it were fair, Pryderi reckons, for the man who did him this wrong to pit his body against his, and let the two hosts stand aside.') [pp.59-60]

Note the use of the word *cam* (wrong) again. We are reminded of the first branch where a similar situation occurred:

'A wyrda,' heb ef [Hafgan], 'ymwerendewch yn da. Y rwng y deu wrenhin y mae yr oet hwnn, a hynny y rwng y deu gorff wylldeu... A ssegur y digaun pawb o honawch uot, eithyr gadu y ryngthunt wylldeu.' [p.5]
('Men,' he said [Hafgan], 'listen carefully. This meeting is between the two kings, and that between their two bodies... and each of you may stand aside, and let the fight be between them.') [p.6]

Pryderi wants compensation, but wishes to seek it himself. In *Branwen* victory is gained by dint of arms; in *Manawydan* patience and a keen mind win the day; here, in *Math,* Gwydion uses magic and enchantment to overcome his opponent:

Ac o nerth grym ac angerd, a hut a lledrith, Guydyon a oruu, a Phryderi a las... [p.73]
(And by dint of strength and valour and by magic and enchantment Gwydion conquered, and Pryderi was slain...) [p.60]

Goewin informs Math that he, too, has been insulted:

'...A threis arnaf a orugant a chywilyd y titheu, a chyscu a wnaethpwyt genhyf, a hynny i'th ystauell ac i'th wely.' [p.74]
('...And they wrought rape upon me and dishonour upon you, and I was lain with, and that in your chamber and your bed.') [p.61]

As Brynley Roberts points out [1980:xix], when a man is insulted not only is his status attacked but also his dignity as a person, causing him *cywilydd* (shame/dishonour). One can seek payment for an insult, but how does one compensate for dishonour? Gwydion and Gilfaethwy eventually appear at court to make amends, but as Math says:

'...Vyg kywilyd ny ellwch chwi y dalu y mi, heb angheu Pryderi...' [p.74]
('...My dishonour you cannot repay me, let alone the death of Pryderi...') [p.61]

Their punishment is to be transformed into animals, male and female, and bear offspring:

'A wyr,' heb ef [Math], 'o gwnaethauch gam ymi, digawn y buawch ym poen, a chywilyd mawr a gawssawch, bot plant o bob un o honawch o'y gilid. . .' [pp.76-77]
('Ah men,' he said [Math], 'if you did me wrong, long enough has been your punishment, and great shame have you had, that each one of you has had young by the other. . .') [p.63]

Math shows us that one cannot make amends for dishonour, one can only forgive:

'A wyr,' heb ef [Math], 'tangneued a gawsawch, a cherennyd a geffwch. . .' [p.77]
('Ah men,' he said [Math], 'you have obtained peace, and you shall have friendship. . .') [p.63]

Lleu, too, suffers dishonour in the fourth branch when Gronw Pebyr sleeps with his wife, Blodeuwedd. According to medieval Welsh law this was a great insult to a married man [Jenkins and Owen 1980: 50-54]. When Lleu's strength is restored, the first thing that comes to his mind is to seek compensation. He is not willing to accept land or gold for the insult, although he shows a little mercy towards Gronw by allowing him to place a stone between himself and the blow. This proves to be of no avail and Gronw is killed on the banks of the river Cynfael. Blodeuwedd, too, is punished, not by her husband but by her creator, Gwydion:

'Ny ladaf i di. Mi a wnaf yssyd waeth it. Sef yw hynny,' heb ef, 'dy ellwng yn rith ederyn. Ac o achaws y kywilyd a wnaethost ti y Lew Llaw Gyffes, na ueidych ditheu dangos dy wyneb lliw dyd byth, a hynny rac ouyn yr holl adar. A bot gelynyaeth y rynghot a'r holl adar. A bot yn anyan udunt dy uaedu, a'th amherchi, y lle i'th gaffant. . .' [p.91]
('I will not slay you. I will do to you that which is worse; that is,' he said, 'I will let you go in the form of a bird. And because of the dishonour you have done to Lleu Llaw Gyffes, you are never to dare show your face in the light of day, and that through fear of all birds. And there will be enmity between you and all the birds, and it will be in their nature to strike and to dishonour you wherever they may find you. . .') [pp.73-74]

There is an interesting use of the verb *maedu* (to strike) here. The same verb is used in the laws to describe the three occasions when a husband is legally permitted to beat his wife:

64

Sef yw y tri pheth hynny y dyly y maedu: am rodi peth ny dylyho y rodi, ac am y chaffel gan wr, ac am unaw meuel ar y uaraf.

(These are the three things for which she should be struck: for giving away goods which she is not entitled to give, for being found with another man, and for swearing shame on his beard.)

[Jenkins and Owen 1980:51 n.37]

I should like to suggest that the author of the fourth branch has chosen the verb intentionally here—the punishment that Lleu should fulfil has now been transmitted to the birds.

Conclusion

It would seem, therefore, that similar themes are apparent in all four branches, namely the nature of insult and compensation, friendship, dishonour and vengeance. Throughout we are aware of the author's emphasis on a moral code of conduct—underneath the magic and enchantment there is a message of lasting significance. As emphasised by Bollard [1983:68]:

the author of *The Mabinogi* has minimized the non-Christian elements of the tales and within his version of these obviously ancient stories he presents a Weltanschauung and an ethos which is of great import and relevance to his contemporary audience and which is not inconsistent with the Judaeo-Christian ethical system within which the audience lives.

5 CHARACTERISATION

This moral code of conduct is reflected in the characters of the *Pedeir Keinc,* in their behaviour towards one another and in the choices they make [Bollard 1983; Valente 1986]. In an oral tale the tendency is for characters to be extremes and to be types. Walter Ong notes that:

> Oral memory works effectively with 'heavy' characters, persons whose deeds are monumental, memorable and commonly public. Thus the noetic economy of its nature generates outsize figures... Colorless personalities cannot survive oral mnemonics. [1982:70]

With the development of the written word, narrative comes to rely less on the heroic and marvellous until eventually it is able to 'move comfortably in the ordinary human lifeworld typical of the novel' [Ong 1982:70]. There is also a tendency for characters to become more complex, in other words their motives and feelings are analysed. In this area we see the author of the *Pedeir Keinc* perhaps beginning to move away from the world of the oral *cyfarwydd*; he carefully delineates his characters and shows a genuine interest in human nature. Yet, the author does not comment on the behaviour of his characters—they express themselves by means of their actions and words.

Pwyll

One could argue that the male characters in *Pedeir Keinc y Mabinogi* make less of an impression on the reader than the women. Pwyll is introduced as a young lord who behaves impatiently towards Arawn. Yet he acknowledges his guilt and offers to make amends. Indeed, he behaves more faithfully than expected by not sleeping with the king's wife, proving himself to be a true friend. In the second part of the branch Pwyll is again portrayed as an impetuous young man, boastful before his men:

> 'Nyt oes arnaf i ouyn cael kymriw, neu archolleu, ym plith hynn o niuer...' [p.9]
> ('I am not afraid to receive wounds or blows among such a host as this...') [p.9]

Rather than seek advice regarding the 'wonder', and weigh up the situation carefully, he does that which comes naturally to him—he acts immediately. Rhiannon shows how such behaviour is foolish, and suggests that more can be done through words than by dint of arms. So the second hunt comes to an end and Pwyll learns another lesson. In the dialogue between Pwyll and Rhiannon the medieval social conventions regarding marriage are turned upside down. As a rule, the girl would play a passive role—she would normally be given to a husband by the male members of her kin in order to unite two families, or as a favour or a gift. Here Rhiannon takes on the male role; she chooses Pwyll and organises the marriage feast herself. In the feast Pwyll again shows his naivety and his indiscretion:

'Pa arch bynnac a erchych di ymi, hyt y gallwyf y gaffael, itti y byd.' [p.14]
('Whatever boon you ask of me, so far as I can get it, it shall be yours.') [p.13]

—although he has learned the power of words in his first meeting with Rhiannon, he has yet to learn how to use words wisely and carefully. But he is given a second chance, and note his care this time in seeking the advice of others:

'A minheu a'e kymmeraf yn llawen,' heb y Pwyll, 'gan gynghor Heueyd a Riannon.' 'Kynghor yw hynny gynnym ni,' heb wynt. 'Y gymryt a wnaf,' heb y Pwyll. [p.17]
('And gladly will I accept it,' said Pwyll, 'with the advice of Hyfaidd and Rhiannon.' 'That is our advice,' they said. 'I accept it,' said Pwyll.) [p.16]

After the marriage Pwyll begins to assert himself. He insists that his wife return to Dyfed with him immediately after the marriage feast, and asks for more time when his men request him to take another wife since he and Rhiannon have no offspring. After his son's disappearance he stands firm:

'Nyt oed achaws ganthunt wy y erchi y mi yscar a'm gwreic namyn na bydei plant idi. Plant a wnn i y uot idi hi. Ac nyt yscaraf a hi. O gwnaeth hitheu gam, kymeret y phenyt amdanaw.' [p.21]
('They had no cause to request me to divorce my wife, save her having no children. I know her to have children. And I will not divorce her. If she has done wrong, let her do penance for it.') [p.19]

This speech combines the lessons which Pwyll has learned—one must pay compensation for every wrong, and one must choose one's words carefully. This time he can get the better of his men because he has observed their words closely—we are reminded of his first unfortunate encounter with Gwawl. One feels that Pendefig Dyfed (Prince of Dyfed) has matured by the end of the branch and fully deserves the name Pwyll (meaning 'discretion' or 'good sense').

Pryderi

There are similarities between Pryderi and his father, Pwyll. He is introduced as a wonder child and his first words in the text reflect his strength and courtesy to his parents as he refuses to allow Rhiannon to carry him to court on her back:

> 'Aet a'y mynho,' heb y mab, 'nyt af i.' [p.25]
> ('Let him go who will,' said the boy, 'I shall not go.') [p.22]

In the third branch we see his extreme generosity for he gives the seven cantrefs of Dyfed to Manawydan. Friendship is important to him as it was to his father, but during his first visit to England we are reminded of Pwyll's impetuous nature as Pryderi insists that the best course of action would be to kill the local craftsmen. Manawydan tries to teach him discretion and wisdom. But in vain, for when his dogs disappear in the enchanted fort, Pryderi follows them. And here greed imprisons him:

> Gorawenu a wnaeth ynteu wrth decket yr eur, a dahet gueith y cawc; a dyuot a wnaeth yn yd oed y cawc, ac ymauael ac ef. [p.56]
> (He rejoiced because of the great beauty of the gold and the good workmanship of the bowl; and he came to where the bowl was and grasped it.) [pp.46-47]

Greed finally causes his death. In the fourth branch Gwydion attempts to steal the pigs of Annwfn from Pryderi who explains:

> 'Ie,' heb ynteu, 'hawssaf yn y byt oed hynny by na bei ammot y rof a'm gwlat amdanunt; sef yw hynny, nat elont y genhyf yny hilyont eu deu kymeint yn y wlat.' [p.69]
> ('Yes,' he said, 'that would be the easiest thing in the world were there not a covenant between me and my country concerning them; that is, that they shall not go from me till they have bred double their number in the land.') [p.57]

He breaks the *ammot* (covenant) because of the attractive bargain offered to him by Gwydion. Pryderi is tricked, it is true, yet Gwydion strikes him in his weak spot and appeals to his greed. The author shows that breaking one's word can lead to destruction and that Pryderi is ultimately responsible for his own destiny. As the men of the South and the men of Gwynedd fight, we almost expect both sides to be destroyed. But Pryderi is not willing for the tragedy that occurred in Ireland to occur a second time. The quarrel is between him and Gwydion, and he requests that they fight alone. We are reminded of the battle between Hafgan and Pwyll, Pryderi's father, at the beginning of the first branch. On that occasion Pwyll was victorious against a king from the Otherworld; this time Gwydion's supernatural powers win the day:

> Ac o nerth grym ac angerd, a hut a lledrith, Guydyon a oruu, a Phryderi a las. . . [p.73]
> (And by dint of strength and valour and by magic and enchantment Gwydion conquered and Pryderi was slain. . .) [p.60]

The suggestion is that the supernatural can only be overcome with the help of an otherworld figure. And was it not a fatal flaw in Pryderi's character that ultimately led to his death?

Bendigeidfran/Brân

In the character of Bendigeidfran we have the portrait of the ideal king, the defender of his kin and country. Like Pwyll at the beginning of the first branch he is determined to make amends for the insult done to Matholwch, and pays much more compensation than is demanded by law. Having heard of Branwen's punishment his natural reaction is to grieve for her, and revenge takes second place. He organises an effective attack on Ireland, leaving behind men to rule the Island of the Mighty in his absence. Having reached Ireland the leader's role is emphasised as Bendigeidfran lies across the river so that his men may walk over him to the other side:

> '. . . a uo penn bit pont. Mi a uydaf pont,' heb ef. [pp.40-41]
> ('. . .he who is chief, let him be a bridge. I will myself be a bridge,' he said.) [p.34]

He succeeds in striking a bargain with the Irish and secures peace between the two countries—he is the ideal statesman. Then, as Efnysien's terrible deed leads to a renewal in the fighting, we have a sensitive portrait of the older brother protecting his sister, grasping her with one hand, and his shield with the other. Even when he is mortally wounded, Bendigeidfran has made preparations for his men, and attempts to secure peace in the land for years to come—his head is to be buried and serve as a talisman:

> A hwnnw trydyd matcud ban gudywyt, a'r trydyd anuat datcud pann datcudywyt; cany doey ormes byth drwy uor y'r ynys honn, tra uei y penn yn y cud hwnnw. [p.47]
> (And when it was buried, that was one of the Three Happy Conceal-ments, and one of the Three Unhappy Disclosures when it was disclosed; for no oppression would ever come across the sea to this island so long as the head was in that concealment.) [p.40]

Matholwch

Throughout the second branch we are aware of a stark contrast between Bendigeidfran and the Irish king, a weak character who is easily influenced. One feels that Matholwch is ruled by his men rather than they by him. After Efnysien has maimed the horses, the reaction of the Irishmen is that this insult was done intentionally. Matholwch is not so sure, but nevertheless he allows his men to lead him and to take decisions on his behalf. This is emphasised a second time as Matholwch relates the story of the cauldron to Bendigeidfran. Matholwch failed to control the strange family that emerged from Llyn y Pair (The Lake of the Cauldron), and the Irishmen forced him to choose between his land and the monstrous family. Matholwch attempted to destroy the family, but they escaped to Wales. The difference between Bendigeidfran and Matholwch is highlighted in the way the family is treated by the king of Britain:

> 'Eu rannu ym pob lle yn y kyuoeth, ac y maent yn lluossauc, ac yn dyrchauael ym pob lle, ac yn cadarnhau y uann y bythont, o wyr ac arueu goreu a welas neb.' [p.36]
> ('I scattered them all over my kingdom, and they are numerous and prosper everywhere, and fortify whatever place they happen to be in with men and arms, the best that any one has seen.') [p.31]

Bendigeidfran channelled their power to his own ends. We have therefore been prepared for Matholwch's reaction to his men when they rise up and demand that Branwen be punished. He is a puppet in the hands of his people, refusing to defend his wife, unlike Pwyll in the first branch. When the Welsh land in Ireland, Matholwch follows the advice of his men yet again and retreats. He greets Bendigeidfran as a kinsman—*cyuathrachwr*—when he asks for peace, reminding us of the purpose of his journey to Wales in the first place:

'Mynnu *ymgyuathrachu* a thidy, Arglwyd...' [p.30]
('He seeks to *ally* himself with you, lord...') [p.26]

—that is, he sought to unite the two families by marriage. Here Matholwch appeals to Bendigeidfran's family ties—they are now one family—and the king of Britain's loyalty to his family has already been proven. The difference between the two kings is again underlined when advice is sought. Bendigeidfran's men realise that there is no bridge over the river Llinon, and they turn to him and ask:

'...Mae dy gynghor am bont?' heb wy.' [p.40]
('...What is your counsel as to a bridge?' they said.) [p.34]

Matholwch, on the other hand, rarely gives advice to his men—when discussing terms of peace, it is Matholwch who is unsure:

'A wyr,' heb y Matholwch, 'mae ych kynghor chwi?' [p.41]
('Ah men,' said Matholwch, 'what is your counsel?') [p.35]

Therefore, by means of Matholwch's character, and by juxtaposing him with Bendigeidfran, it would seem that the author is trying to say something about the nature of kingship and about the responsibilities that belong to that office.

Efnysien

Efnysien is the most complex character in *Branwen*—he is the catalyst in the first and the second part of the branch. He is insulted as the Welsh give his sister to Matholwch without his permission, but the fact that he mutilates the horses in a cruel way, rather than kill them, reflects the perverted nature of his character. A further suggestion of his abnormality is seen when he scans the house built for Bendigeidfran 'with fierce, ruthless eyes' [p.36], and when he proceeds to kill the Irishmen in the sacks by squeezing their heads until he feels his fingers sink into the brain through the bone. It is almost as if he enjoys such torture, and takes pleasure from shocking people:

'Y Duw y dygaf uyg kyffes,' heb ynteu yn y uedwl, 'ys anhebic a gyflauan gan y tylwyth y wneuthur, a wnaf i yr awr honn.' A chyuodi y uynyd, a chymryt y mab erwyd y traet, a heb ohir, na chael o dyn yn

71

y ty gauael arnaw, yny want y mab yn wysc y benn yn y gynneu. [p.43] ('By my confession to God,' he said in his mind, 'a crime the household would not think might be committed is the crime I shall now commit.' And he got up, and took the boy by the feet, and without delay, nor did a man in the house get hold of him before he thrust the boy headlong into the blazing fire.) [pp.36-37]

We do not get to know Efnysien by means of dialogue but through his actions and through his short monologues. Note again the author's attention to detail and how he suggests this character's sinister nature by causing him to say things 'in his mind' rather than openly to other people, in other words he is a character who keeps everything to himself and acts without consultation. He is a lonely figure and evil is an inherent part of his nature. Yet, he repents and tries to make amends for his wicked deeds by destroying the cauldron, and in so doing breaks his own heart; Branwen, too, breaks her heart on her return to Wales. In an ironic way, therefore, brother and sister are united in the manner of their death.

Manawydan

When Manawydan is described at the beginning of the third branch he is presented as a weak and wretched man, full of grief and longing as he laments his own sad fate. Lamenting has always traditionally been regarded as the domain of the female, and there is a striking similarity between this description of Manawydan and that of Branwen mourning at the end of the second branch. Manawydan is a modest man who never once claimed land or territory. We would expect him to fight against Caswallon and avenge the wrong done to his brother, Bendigeidfran. But it is clear that the author in this branch intends to discuss different values, and he does this by means of Manawydan's character. Indeed, many have argued that the author has chosen Manawydan as the exponent of his own personal philosophy [Mac Cana 1977:56-60; Lloyd 1974:36-39. But compare Koch 1987]. Pryderi gives him land and a wife, and once re-established in society his self-confidence grows. It is he who takes the lead when the enchantment falls on Dyfed, and he, too, suggests making for England to seek a livelihood. Manawydan guides Pryderi and teaches him various crafts. Throughout the branch his wisdom and patience are emphasised, providing a sharp contrast to Pryderi's impatience. An insight into the cautious nature of his character has already been given in the second branch as he draws the attention of his companions to the door facing Cornwall:

> 'Weldy racco,' heb y Manawydan, 'y drws ny dylywn ni y agori.' [p.46]
> ('See yonder,' said Manawydan, 'the door we must not open.') [p.39]

In the second part of the third branch Manawydan's loyalty is apparent, and also his determination. Cigfa's entreaties have no effect on him, although the just and fair traits in his nature are emphasised as he says to her:

> 'Bei gwypwn inheu defnyd yn y byt y dylyut titheu bot yn borth idaw ef, mi a uydwn wrth dy gynghor am danaw; a chanys gwnn, Arglwydes, medwl yw genhyf y diuetha.' [p.61]
> ('If I knew of any reason in the world why you should help it [i.e. the mouse], I would abide by your counsel concerning it; but as I know of none, lady, I intend to destroy it.') [p.50]

Note the subtle use of the word *Arglwydes* [Lady] here—this is the only time Manawydan addresses Cigfa in this way. Manawydan's courtesy is therefore emphasised as he disagrees with the lady. We see again the importance of justice in Manawydan's eyes as he insists on hanging the mouse, the lawful penalty for stealing. In other words, he wishes to adhere to the letter of the law and act within the legal system. He cannot be bribed with gold, silver and horses—his loyalty to his friend and his wife is worth much more than this. At the end of the branch Manawydan—and the author—show that more can be attained by means of fair words than by the sword, an idea that is explored further in the Romances as King Arthur says of Gwalchmai:

> 'Mi a wydwn na bydei reit y Walchmei ymlad a'r marchawc. A diryfed yw idaw kaffel clot. Mwy a wna ef o'e eireu tec no nini o nerth an harueu.' [Goetinck 1976: 35]
> ('I knew Gwalchmai would not need to fight with the knight. Nor is it to be wondered at that he has won renown. He does more with his fair words than we by dint of our arms.) [p.202]

Math

Math, in the fourth branch of the *Mabinogi* is presented as a fair and just ruler. We see him, too, attempting to distance himself from the heroic ethos in which fighting plays such an essential part:

'. . . Ni chymellaf inheu ar neb uynet e ymlad, dros wneuthur ohanam ninheu an gallu.' [p.73]
('. . . I will not compel any one to go to fight, instead of our doing what we can.') [p.60]

Having discovered that Gwydion and Gilfaethwy have betrayed him, his first care is for Goewin and for her well-being. He then punishes the two brothers but forgives them when they have paid their debt and offers them his friendship once more. He goes even further than this and shows that he has faith in them once again by asking their advice regarding a new virgin foot-holder. Further proof of his magnanimous nature is his gift of Cantref Dinodig to Lleu, 'the very best cantref for a young man to have' [p.68]. He helps Gwydion to create a wife for his nephew, and at the end of the branch his men, the men of Gwynedd, help Lleu to overcome Gronw Pebyr. Math is therefore presented as an ideal king. But he is far less removed from his traditional sources than many of the other characters—he is a sorcerer with the power to transform men into beasts.

Gwydion

At Math's side is Gwydion who often uses his supernatural powers to promote evil. He succeeds in tricking Math and obtains his permission to journey to Dyfed and seek Pryderi's pigs. He succeeds in winning the admiration and friendship of Pryderi by his skill at storytelling and conversing, until the lord of Dyfed admits:

'Tauawt lawn da yw y teu di.' [p.69]
('A right good tongue is yours.') [p.57]

It is Gwydion's ability to talk and appeal to the avaricious element in Pryderi's character that leads ultimately to the downfall of the hero. Having overcome Pryderi by using magic and enchantment, Gwydion asks Math to free the hostage given to Gwynedd by the men of Dyfed. He is not showing any remorse here; rather he wants to ensure that Math will not come to learn of the reason for the strife. So at the beginning of the fourth branch Gwydion is portrayed as a character who has no principles whatsoever, although it could be argued that his main aim in all of this was to help his brother Gilfaethwy. His solution, however, imperils all of Gwynedd and brings about Goewin's violation [Valente 1986:245]. After his punishment and the birth of Lleu, he acts to secure a name, arms and a wife for his nephew. We see the depth of his love towards Lleu after the young man's disappearance—Gwydion is determined not to rest until he finds him. The tragedy is that his own creation—Blodeuwedd—was partly responsible for events. At the end of the tale we have a portrait of a magician unable to control his own creation—his supernatural power has reacted against him, bringing shame to the man he loved most. Rather than kill Blodeuwedd he transforms her into an owl, just as he and his brother were transformed into animals at the beginning of the tale. We have, therefore, moved in a complete circle; Gwydion the magician now plays the part of the judge and has learned how to differentiate between right and wrong.

Gronw

Gronw is portrayed as an unpleasant coward. It is he who makes the first move in his relationship with Blodeuwedd by approaching the court at dusk. The ruler of a court was expected to be generous and welcoming, so Blodeuwedd feels obliged to invite him in:

> 'Dioer,' heb hi, 'ni a gawn yn goganu gan yr unben o'e adu y prytwn y wlat arall, onys guahodwn.' [p.84]
> ('God knows,' she said, 'we shall be ill-spoken of by the chieftain for letting him go at this hour to another domain, if we do not ask him in.') [p.69]

Having declared their love for each other, Gronw advises Blodeuwedd what to do regarding her husband:

> 'Nyt oes gynghor it,' heb ef, 'onyt un; keissaw y ganthaw gwybot pa furu y del y angheu, a hynny yn rith ymgeled amdanaw.' [p.85]
> ('There is no counsel for you,' he said, 'save one; to seek to learn from him how his death may come about, and that under pretence of loving care for him.') [p.69]

—and as he finally takes his leave, he reminds her yet again:

> '...coffa a dywedeis wrthyt, ac ymdidan yn lut ac ef; a hynny yn rith ysmalawch caryat ac ef. A dilyt y gantaw pa ford y gallei dyuot y angheu.' [p.86]
> ('...remember what I told you, and speak closely with him, and that under pretence of importunity of love of him. And draw from him what way his death might come about.') [p.70]

Therefore, the author shows Gronw planting the idea in Blodeuwedd's mind and advising her exactly as to how to discover Lleu's secret. At the end of the branch his cowardice is apparent; he offers land and money to Lleu as compensation; then he enquires among his retinue if there is anyone willing to accept the blow on his behalf. The retinue or *comitatus* was expected to be loyal to its leader (compare the men of Mynyddog Mwynfawr described in the sixth century *Gododdin* poem who fought to their death), sacrificing all. Gronw's men, therefore, show the utmost disrespect by turning their back on their leader. And even at the end, Gronw persists with his pleading; he asks for a stone to be placed between him and the blow, and accuses Blodeuwedd of having tricked him:

> 'Arglwyd,' heb ef, 'canys o drycystryw gwreic y gwneuthum yti a wneuthum. . . .' [p.92]
> ('Lord,' he said, 'since it was through a woman's wiles I did to you that which I did. . .') [p.74]

Gronw Pebyr is presented as a despicable character, as dishonourable in life as in death.

Rhiannon

Although the male characters of *Pedeir Keinc y Mabinogi* are interesting, it is probably the females who are most memorable [Valente 1986]. Rhiannon is a strong character, fighting against contemporary social order and marrying a man of her own choice. She is totally fearless at her first meeting with Pwyll—she stands and waits for him, uncovers her face, fixes her gaze upon him and begins to converse with him. She plays the active role in the courtship and shows her lack of patience with Pwyll as he destroys her plans in the first wedding feast:

> 'Taw, hyt y mynnych,' heb y Riannon, 'ny bu uuscrellach gwr ar y ssynnwyr e hun nog ry uuost ti.' [p.14]
> ('Be dumb as long as you will,' said Rhiannon, 'never was there a man made feebler use of his wits than you have.') [p.13]

At the end of the second feast she is responsible for drawing up the terms of peace, and on the morning following their marriage she commands her husband to 'rise and begin to content the minstrels' [p.16]. We are reminded of a similar command she gave to Gwawl, encouraging him to get inside Pwyll's magic bag [p.15]. By using similar phrases the author reminds us of Gwawl's blindness and of the power that Rhiannon has over men. However, it seems that this power does not extend over women too, for after her son's disappearance she cannot persuade the six women to tell the truth about the incident. Suddenly Rhiannon is no longer in control of the situation; she knows that there is no point quarrelling with the women and accepts her penance stoically. When her son is returned to her, note her sensitivity as Pwyll gives him the name Pryderi:

> 'Edrychwch,' heb y Riannon, 'na bo goreu y gueda arnaw y enw e hun.' [p.26]
> ('See,' said Rhiannon, 'lest his own name does not become him best.') [p.23]

In these words she extends her sympathy to Teyrnon's wife who will now revert to being childless. In the third branch, Rhiannon is given to a man for the second time and there is no opposition on her behalf. Her son describes her in an affectionate manner when he tells Manawydan:

> 'Mi a debygaf na werendeweist eiryoet ar ymdidanwreic well no hi. Er amser y bu hitheu yn y dewred, ny bu wreic delediwach no hi, ac etwa ny bydy anuodlawn y phryt.' [p.50]
> ('I am sure that you never listened to a better conversationalist than she. When she was in her prime, no lady was more beautiful than she, and even now you shall not be ill-pleased with her looks.') [p.42]

It would seem that Rhiannon loses her supernatural and independent traits after marrying Pwyll, that is after being assimilated into a mortal world. But we are reminded of her sharp tongue in the third branch as she rebukes Manawydan for leaving Pryderi in the magic fort. On this occasion we see that Rhiannon's love towards her son is so blind that it causes her to behave rashly and lose control, and we are reminded of the other occasion when her son was lost and of the anguish she suffered.

Branwen

It has already been noted that the branches have no titles in the manuscripts and that they were first published in Lady Charlotte Guest's translation of the *Mabinogion*. This is significant as regards the second branch, for it has been given the title *Branwen uerch Lyr. Pwyll* and *Math* have been named after the *incipit,* a common practice with medieval texts as noted by Walter Ong [1982:125]:

> Manuscript culture had preserved a feeling for a book as a kind of utterance, an occurrence in the course of conversation, rather than as an object. Lacking title pages and often titles, a book from pre-print,

77

manuscript culture is normally catalogued by its 'incipit' (a Latin verb meaning 'it begins'), or the first words of its text (referring to the Lord's Prayer as the 'Our Father' is referring to it by its incipit and evinces a certain residual orality).

The third branch does not have the usual opening formula, but since Manawydan is so obviously the central character in the tale, it seems reasonable to name the branch after him. The second branch begins with the *incipit Bendigeiduran uab Llyr* and one would expect this title to be given to the second branch. Indeed, *Brân* is the title given to the branch by William Owen-Pughe in his translation of the *Mabinogi*, a translation that was never published, but that preceded Guest's work by some thirty years [Davies 1990]. It would seem, therefore, that Charlotte Guest was the first to use *Branwen* as a title for the second branch. Therefore, because of the current title, perhaps more attention has been paid to Branwen's character than the author intended. After all, a title greatly influences our approach to a work and our interpretation of it.

Branwen is a passive character at the beginning of the branch—she is given by her family to Matholwch for political reasons, and goes off to Ireland obediently. The author paints her as the ideal woman—she is the most beautiful maiden in the world, and is also extremely generous as reflected in her behaviour on her arrival in Ireland. After she has fulfilled her obligation and given Matholwch a son, she is punished for Efnysien's malicious deed. Her patience is reflected in the words:

Blwynyded nit llei no their, y buant yuelly. [p.38]
(Not less than three years they continued in that way.) [p.32]

—and the careful, thorough way she goes about rearing the starling. Many scholars have drawn attention to her keen reply as Matholwch's men ask her:

'Arglwydes... beth dybygy di yw hynny?' [p.40]
('Lady... what do you suppose that is?') [pp.33-34]

and she reminds them that they no longer treat her as a lady:

'Kyn ny bwyf Arglwydes,' heb hi, 'mi a wnn beth yw hynny...'
[p.40]
('Although I am no lady,' she said, 'I know what that is...') [p.34]

78

She explains that the vision they have seen is Bendigeidfran and his men crossing over from the Island of the Mighty, and ends with an excellent example of litotes as befits her character:

'Ef,' heb hi, 'yn edrych ar yr ynys honn, llidyawc yw...' [p.40]
('He,' she said, 'looking at this island, he is angry...') [p.34]

Branwen is presented as a peacemaker as she advises her brother to accept Matholwch's offer, 'and lest the land be laid to waste she did that' [p.35]. We see here her loyalty to the Irish, even after they have treated her so cruelly—she now has ties with both countries, as symbolised by her son Gwern. Although Efnysien is responsible for the ensuing destruction, Branwen takes the blame, claiming that two islands have been laid waste because of her. In death she is calm and noble, as in life:

A dodi ucheneit uawr, a thorri y chalon ar hynny. [p.45]
(And she heaved a great sigh, and with that broke her heart.) [p.38]

Blodeuwedd

Blodeuwedd is the unfaithful wife of the fourth. branch. She is conjured up out of flowers to overcome Aranrhod's third curse. It is true that she deceives Lleu, but as has been argued previously, Gronw advises her, and gives her detailed instructions. The bedroom scene, with Blodeuwedd attempting to discover Lleu's secret, is reminiscent of the scene between Arawn and his wife in the first branch, after his return to Annwfn. The chastity of Arawn's wife is the concern in *Pwyll*; here it is Blodeuwedd's infidelity. At the end of the branch, Blodeuwedd is a frightened girl, running away to the mountains with her maidens until she is finally caught and punished for breaking the social code. As Jean Markale has suggested [1980:147-172], she is the Eve of the *Mabinogi*—both women were created specially for their husbands and had no choice in the matter. Lleu and Blodeuwedd are given some sort of an earthly paradise by Math and they live happily within the narrow, patriarchal idea of happiness, as a married couple. Then the pattern is destroyed by the sexual love of the wife and the young hero Gronw. One can interpret the episode on another level and argue that committing adultery was a symbolic act in Blodeuwedd's eyes. The important thing was to rebel against patriarchal and matrimonial authority, to run away from her creator (Gwydion) and her owner (Lleu). And the way to cause greatest pain to Lleu was by committing adultery. Gronw and Blodeuwedd could have kept their love secret, but by attempting to kill Lleu the rebellion was complete. Blodeuwedd is unsuccessful—Gwydion uses magic and enchantment to restore order. One could argue, therefore, that this is no ordinary adultery but rather a wife who wishes to control her own personality and freedom to use her intellect and emotions as she chooses. It has been seen, throughout *Pedeir Keinc y Mabinogi*, how a girl's social status is dependent on the status of her nearest male kin, in accordance with medieval Welsh law. The majority of women in the *Pedeir Keinc* are named according to their relationship with their father or husband, for example Rhiannon daughter of Hyfaidd Hen, Cigfa daughter of Gwynn Gohoyw, Branwen daughter of Llyr. Personal names are not even given to the wife of Arawn, Teyrnon and Llwyd. It was the men's role to defend their women, and great emphasis was placed on safeguarding the girl's honour, before and after marriage. Great emphasis was also placed on virginity before marriage, as reflected in the tales of Goewin and Aranrhod. Blodeuwedd therefore rebels against these standards. But the author shows that no good can come out of such antisocial behaviour—Gronw is killed and Blodeuwedd is transformed into an owl.

Conclusion

Throughout *Pedeir Keinc y Mabinogi*, therefore, the author uses his characters to reinforce his ideas regarding proper social conduct. The virtues to be fostered are patience, modesty, wisdom, chastity, loyalty,—these are the virtues that will ultimately win the day. As emphasised by Mac Cana [1977:60]:

> In his narrative and use of character, particularly in the case of Manawydan, he subtly conveys a scale of values which, by implication, he commends to the practice of contemporary society. For the exaggerated and impulsive ideals of heroic tradition—and, one suspects, of much of contemporary life—he projects the more Christian and more practical virtues of patience and compromise.

6 CONCLUSION

It has not been the intention of this discussion to analyse the possible origin and development of *Pedeir Keinc y Mabinogi*. Rather, the approach has been a synchronic one—the emphasis has been on the tales as they stand. The general themes have been examined, together with characterisation. It has been argued that we are dealing with an author to whom a moral code of conduct was important, a man who placed great emphasis on friendship and on peace. He used tales and traditions from the past as a medium for his ideas, and commended to his contemporary audience a certain ethical system. His greatest achievement was his characterisation—here we see most clearly, perhaps, his genius and his own personal creative talent. On the other hand, it has been argued that this was a man steeped in the narrative techniques of traditional storytelling. The structure of the tales is episodic, while symmetrical composition may also have played a part. Moreover, tripartite structure and redundancy are common features within the narrative. The style of the written texts betrays an oral influence. The emphasis throughout is on a chronological order and additive style. Dialogue plays an essential part, together with speech markers. Indeed, these are features that many scholars have shown to be characteristic of oral texts. I have also argued that the author was drawing on a stock of traditional verbal patterns or formulae, again a technique associated with oral performance. The theory is, therefore, that the conventions of the *cyfarwydd* have greatly influenced the author, and that the art of the oral storyteller has left its mark on the written tales.

Pedeir Keinc y Mabinogi are regarded as one of the classics of Welsh literature. The author is a gifted writer who has drawn on the oral tradition for the basis of his style and material, yet has used such resources to his own literary ends. His strength lies in his attention to detail (reflected in his precise use of words), his careful delineation of character, his skilful use of dialogue—indeed, he is a master of Welsh prose. He succeeds in varying the tempo and dramatic intensity of his narrative, and presents us with an ever-changing canvas of events. He is not concerned with rhetorical embellishments or hyperbole—his writing is economical and suggestive rather than descriptive. Through his prose he tells a series of exciting and dramatic stories.

Mortals come into contact with otherworld powers, and magic and enchantment are part of every day life. But the tales are also imbued with the author's own ideals and values, and this sets them apart from most other Welsh tales of the medieval period. A deep and genuine interest in humanity is apparent, and the author's personal voice is clearly audible.

Just as traditional stories inspired the author of *Pedeir Keinc y Mabinogi,* so too have the Four Branches, in their turn, inspired contemporary Welsh writers and poets —Saunders Lewis, for example, wrote two plays entitled *Blodeuwedd* and *Branwen*; R. Williams Parry made use of the second branch in his poem *Drudwy Branwen* as did Gwenallt in *Adar Rhiannon.* English-language writers have also turned to the *Mabinogi* for inspiration, including Anthony Conran, Gillian Clarke and Alan Garner. In each case the modern authors have interpreted the tales according to their own personal vision. This is definite proof of their lasting significance and resonance.

REFERENCES

Basgöz, Ilhan 1978. 'Formula in Prose Narrative *Hikaye.*' *Folklore Preprint Series,* 6:1-25.
Bollard, J.K. 1975. 'The Structure of the Four Branches of the Mabinogi.' *Transactions of the Honourable Society of Cymmrodorion:*250-276.
    1980-81. 'Traddodiad a Dychan yn *Breuddwyd Rhonabwy'.* *Llên Cymru,* 13:155-63.
    1983. 'The Role of Myth and Tradition in *The Four Branches of the Mabinogi.'* *Cambridge Medieval Celtic Studies,* 6:67-86.
Bromwich, Rachel 1974. 'Traddodiad Llafar y Chwedlau'. In *Y Traddodiad Rhyddiaith yn yr Oesau Canol.* Ed. by Geraint Bowen. Llandysul: Gomer. pp. 146-75.
    1978. Ed. and trans., *Trioedd Ynys Prydein.* 2nd ed. Cardiff: Wales University Press.
Bruford, Alan 1969. *Gaelic Folk-Tales and Mediaeval Romances.* Dublin: The Folklore of Ireland Society.
Charles-Edwards, Gifford 1979-80. 'The Scribes of the Red Book of Hergest.' *National Library of Wales Journal,* 21:246-56.
Charles-Edwards, T.M. 1970. 'The Date of the Four Branches of the Mabinogi.' *Transactions of the Honourable Society of Cymmrodorion:*263-98.
    1978. 'Honour and Status in Some Irish and Welsh Prose Tales.' *Ériu,* 29:123-42.
Clover, Carol J. 1986. 'The Long Prose Form.' *Arkiv för Nordisk Filologi,* 101:10-39.
Davies, Sioned 1988a. 'Pryd a Gwedd yn y *Mabinogion'.* In *Ysgrifau Beirniadol.* Volume 14. Ed. by J. E. Caerwyn Williams. Denbigh: Gee. pp. 115-33.
    1988b. 'Y Fformiwla yn *Pedeir Keinc y Mabinogi.'* In *Ysgrifau Beirniadol.* Volume 15. pp. 47-72.
    1990. 'Ail Gainc y *Mabinogi*—Llais y Ferch.' In *Ysgrifau Beirniadol.* Volume 17. pp. 15-27.
    1992. 'Storytelling in Medieval Wales.' *Oral Tradition,* 7/2: 231-57..
Delargy, J.H. 1945. 'The Gaelic Story-Teller.' *Proceedings of the British Academy,* 31: 172-221.
Dorson, Richard M. 1960. 'Oral Styles of American Folk Narrators.' In *Style in Language.* Ed. by Thomas A. Sebeok. Cambridge Mass.: M.I.T.Press. pp. 27-51.
Ellis, T.P. 1928. 'Legal References, Terms and Conceptions in the Mabinogion.' *Y Cymmrodor,* 39:86-148.
Evans, J. Gwenogvryn 1907. Ed., *Llyfr Gwyn Rhydderch.* Cardiff: Wales University Press.
Evans, W.L. 1960. 'An Examination of Narrative Methods employed in selected medieval Welsh texts.' B.Litt. diss., Oxford University.
Finnegan, Ruth H. 1990. 'What is Oral Literature Anyway? Comments in the Light of Some African and Other Comparative Material.' In *Oral-Formulaic Theory.* Ed. by John M. Foley. New York: Garland. pp. 243-82.
Ford, Patrick K. 1975-76. 'The Poet as *Cyfarwydd* in Early Welsh Tradition.' *Studia Celtica,* 10-11:152-62.
    1977. *The Mabinogi and Other Medieval Welsh Tales.* Berkeley: University of California Press.

83

Goetinck, Glenys Witchard 1976. Ed., *Historia Peredur vab Efrawc*. Cardiff: Wales University Press.

1988. '*Pedair Cainc y Mabinogi*: Yr Awdur a'i Bwrpas.' *Llên Cymru*, 15:249-269.

Gray, Bennison 1971. 'Repetition in Oral Literature.' *Journal of American Folklore*, 84:289-303.

Green, Miranda 1986. *The Gods of the Celts*. Gloucester: Alan Sutton.

1992. *Dictionary of Celtic Myth and Legend*. London: Thames and Hudson.

Gruffydd, W.J. 1953. *Rhiannon. An Inquiry into the First and Third Branches of the Mabinogi*. Cardiff: Wales University Press.

1958. *Folklore and Myth in the Mabinogion*. Cardiff: Wales University Press.

Guest, Charlotte 1849. Trans., *The Mabinogion*. 3 vols. London: Longmans, Brown, Green and Longmans.

Gwyndaf, Robin 1989. *Welsh Folk Tales*. Cardiff: National Museum of Wales.

Hamp, Eric P. 1975. 'Mabinogi.' *Transactions of the Honourable Society of Cymmrodorion*: 243-249.

Huws, Daniel 1991. 'Llyfr Gwyn Rhydderch'. *Cambridge Medieval Celtic Studies*, 21:1-37.

James, Christine 1991. 'Ym Myd y Mabinogi.' *Barn*, 345:36-38.

Jenkins, Dafydd and Morfydd E. Owen 1980. Eds., *The Welsh Law of Women*. Cardiff: Wales University Press.

Jenkins, Dafydd 1986. Ed. and trans., *The Law of Hywel Dda*. Llandysul: Gomer.

Jones, Glyn E. 1976. 'Early Prose: The Mabinogi.' In *A Guide to Welsh Literature*. Volume I. Ed. by A.O.H. Jarman and G.R. Hughes. Swansea: Christopher Davies. pp. 189-202.

Jones, Gwyn, and Thomas Jones 1949. Trans., *The Mabinogion*. London: Everyman. [I have amended their translation in some instances—S.D.]

Jones, R.M. 1986. 'Narrative Structure in Medieval Welsh Prose Tales.' In *Proceedings of the Seventh International Congress of Celtic Studies*. Ed. by D. Ellis Evans, John G. Griffith and E. M. Jope. Oxford: D. Ellis Evans, Jesus College. pp. 171-198.

Jones, Thomas 1941. Ed., *Brut y Tywysogyon*. Cardiff: Wales University Press.

Kellogg, Robert L. 1991. 'Literary Aesthetics in Oral Art.' *Oral Tradition*, 6:137-40.

Koch, John T. 1987. 'A Welsh Window on the Iron Age: Manawydan, Mandubracios'. *Cambridge Medieval Celtic Studies*, 14:17-52.

Lapidge, Michael 1973-74. 'The Welsh-Latin Poetry of Sulien's Family.' *Studia Celtica*, 8-9:68-106.

Lewis, Saunders 1932. *Braslun o Hanes Llenyddiaeth Gymraeg*. Cardiff: Wales University Press.

Loomis, R.S. 1956. *Wales and the Arthurian Legend*. Cardiff: Wales University Press.

Lord, Albert B. 1960. *The Singer of Tales*. Cambridge Mass.: Harvard University Press.

Lloyd, D. Myrddin 1974. 'Gwareiddiad Cymru yn yr Oesau Canol.' In *Y Traddodiad Rhyddiaith yn yr Oesau Canol*. Ed. by Geraint Bowen. Llandysul: Gomer. pp. 13-45.

Lloyd-Morgan, Ceridwen 1981. 'Narrative Structure in Peredur.' *Zeitschrift für Celtische Philologie*, 38:187-231.

Mac Cana, Proinsias 1958. *Branwen Daughter of Llŷr*. Cardiff: Wales University Press.

1977. *The Mabinogi*. Cardiff: Wales University Press.

1980. *The Learned Tales of Medieval Ireland.* Dublin: Dublin Institute for Advanced Studies.

1983. *Celtic Mythology.* London: Newnes.

Markale, Jean 1980. *Women of the Celts.* Trans. by A. Mygind, C. Hauch and P. Henry. London: Gordon Cremonesi. First French ed. 1972.

Middleton, Roger 1976. 'Studies in the Textual Relationships of the Erec/Gereint Stories.' D. Phil. diss., Oxford University.

Morgan, T.J. 1951. *Ysgrifau Llenyddol.* London: W. Griffiths.

Nutt, Alfred 1910. Notes to Charlotte Guest trans., *The Mabinogion.* London: David Nutt.

Okpewho, Isidore 1977. 'Does the Epic Exist in Africa? Some Formal Considerations.' *Research in African Literatures,* 8:171-200.

Olrik, A. 1965. 'Epic Laws of Folk Narrative.' In *The Study of Folklore.* Ed. by A. Dundes. Englewood Cliffs, NJ: Prentice-Hall. pp. 129-141.

O'Nolan, Kevin 1975. 'The Use of Formula in Story-Telling.' In *Hereditas.* Ed. by Bo Almqvist, Breandán Mac Aodha, Gearóid Mac Eoin. Dublin: The Folklore of Ireland Society. pp. 233-50.

1978. 'Doublets in the *Odyssey.*' *The Classical Quarterly,* 28:23-37.

Ong, Walter J. 1982. *Orality and Literacy.* London: Methuen.

Owen, Morfydd 1974. 'Y Cyfreithiau.' In *Y Traddodiad Rhyddiaith yn yr Oesau Canol.* Ed. by Geraint Bowen. Llandysul: Gomer. pp.196-244.

Parry, Milman 1971. *The Making of Homeric Verse: the Collected Papers of Milman Parry.* Ed. by A. Parry. Oxford: Clarendon Press.

Rhŷs, John 1901. *Celtic Folklore.* Volume I. Oxford: Oxford University Press.

Roberts, Brynley F. 1980. Intro. to Dafydd Ifans and Rhiannon Ifans trans., *Y Mabinogion.* Llandysul: Gomer.

1984. 'From Traditional Tale to Literary Story: Middle Welsh Prose Narratives.' In *The Craft of Fiction.* Ed. by Leigh A. Arrathoon. Rochester: Solaris Press. pp. 211-30.

1986. 'Tales and Romances.' In *A Guide to Welsh Literature.* Volume I. Ed. by A.O.H. Jarman and G.R. Hughes. Swansea: Christopher Davies. pp. 203-43.

1988. 'Oral Tradition and Welsh Literature: A Description and Survey.' *Oral Tradition,* 3:61-87.

Robson, C.A. 1961. 'The Technique of Symmetrical Composition in Medieval Narrative Poetry.' In *Studies in Medieval French.* Ed. by E.A. Francis. Oxford: Oxford University Press. pp. 26-75.

Rosenberg, Bruce A. 1981. 'Oral Literature in the Middle Ages.' In *Oral Traditional Literature.* Ed. by John M. Foley. Columbus, OH: Slavica. pp. 440-50.

1990. 'The Message of the American Folk Sermon.' In *Oral-Formulaic Theory.* Ed. by John M. Foley. New York: Garland. pp. 137-68.

Russo, J.A. 1976. 'Is "Oral" or "Aural" Composition the Cause of Homer's Formulaic Style?' In *Oral Literature and the Formula.* Ed. by B.A. Stolz and R.S. Shannon. Ann Arbor: Center for the Coördination of Ancient and Modern Studies, University of Michigan. pp. 31-48.

Sims-Williams, Patrick 1977-8. 'Riddling Treatment of the "Watchman Device" in *Branwen* and *Togail Bruidne Da Derga.*' *Studia Celtica,* 12-13:83-117.

1982. 'The evidence for vernacular Irish literary influence on early mediaeval Welsh literature'. In *Ireland in Early Mediaeval Europe: Studies in Memory of Kathleen*

Hughes. Ed. by Dorothy Whitelock et al. Cambridge: Cambridge University Press. pp. 235-257.

1991. 'The Submission of Irish Kings in Fact and Fiction: Henry II, Bendigeidfran, and the Dating of *The Four Branches of the Mabinogi.*' *Cambridge Medieval Celtic Studies,* 22:31-61.

Slotkin, Edgar M. 1991. 'The Oral Hypothesis of Medieval Celtic Literatures.' Delivered at the International Congress of Celtic Studies, Paris (unpublished).

Stephens, Thomas 1876. *The Literature of the Kymry*. 2nd ed. London: Longmans.

Tannen, Deborah 1982. 'Oral and Literate Strategies in Spoken and Written Narratives.' *Language,* 58:1-21.

Thomson, R.L. 1968. Ed., *Owein*. Dublin: The Dublin Institute for Advanced Studies.

Tristram, Hildegard 1989. 'Early Modes of Insular Expression.' In *Sages, Saints and Storytellers*. Ed. by D. O Coráin, L. Breatnach, K. Mac Cone. Maynooth: An Sagant. pp. 427-448.

Valente, R.L. 1986. '*Merched y Mabinogi*: Women and the Thematic Structure of the Four Branches.' Ph.D.diss., Cornell University.

Welsh, Andrew 1988. 'The Traditional Narrative Motifs of *The Four Branches of the Mabinogi.*' *Cambridge Medieval Celtic Studies,* 15:51-62.

Williams, Glanmor 1976. *The Welsh Church from Conquest to Reformation*. Cardiff: Wales University Press.

Williams, G.J. and E.J.Jones 1934. Eds., *Gramadegau'r Penceirddiaid*. Cardiff: Wales University Press.

Williams, Ifor 1930. Ed., *Pedeir Keinc y Mabinogi*. Cardiff: Wales University Press.

Williams, S.J. and J.E.Powell 1961. Eds., *Cyfreithiau Hywel Dda yn ôl Llyfr Blegywryd*. 2nd ed. Cardiff: Wales University Press.